# Big Book of
# Knitted Shawls

# DEDICATION

To all the shawl makers out there, thank you.

## Big Book of Knitted Shawls

Landauer Publishing, www.landauerpub.com, is an imprint of Fox Chapel Publishing Company, Inc.

Copyright © 2024 by Jen Lucas and Fox Chapel Publishing Company, Inc.

*Big Book of Knitted Shawls* contains content first published in the following books: *Sock-Yarn Shawls*, *Sock-Yarn Shawls II*, *Sock-Yarn Accessories*, *Cozy Stash-Busting Knits*, and *Stunning Stitches*.

Project Team
Managing Editor: Gretchen Bacon
Acquisitions Editor: Amelia Johanson
Copy Editor: Christa Oestreich
Designer: Matthew Hartsock
Indexer: Jean Bissell

Shutterstock used: ColorMaker (background throughout), New Africa (9, top right).

ISBN 978-1-63981-096-3

Library of Congress Control Number: 2024938138

To learn more about the other great books from Fox Chapel Publishing, or to find a retailer near you, call toll-free 800-457-9112, send mail to 903 Square Street, Mount Joy, PA 17552, or visit us at www.FoxChapelPublishing.com.

We are always looking for talented authors. To submit an idea, please send a brief inquiry to acquisitions@foxchapelpublishing.com.

Printed in China
First printing

# Big Book of
# Knitted
# Shawls

### 35 Patterns in a Variety of Beautiful Yarns, Styles, and Stitches

Landauer Publishing

**Jen Lucas**

# Table of Contents

# Introduction

When I began working on my first book, *Sock-Yarn Shawls*, in 2009, I had no idea what was in store for me. I was a relatively new designer, working a full-time job completely unrelated to the craft industry, and I was trying to decide what I really wanted out of a career. I never thought I would be here, 15 years later, presenting you with a book that brings together a collection of patterns from my previous books.

I've been so fortunate to get to meet so many of you over the years at local yarn shops, festivals, and conventions. Seeing you in class having that "a-ha" moment about a technique or design element is what motivates me to bring you more shawl goodness. I've received many messages over the years from you, sharing your finished project and letting me know who you made it for, along with the hopes, dreams, thoughts, and prayers that you put into each stitch. It's what keeps me going and what draws me back to shawls over and over again.

I am so thankful to all the knitters and crocheters out there who have supported me and my small business—it's because of you I was able to make this book—to keep some of these shawl patterns out there in the world a little bit longer. I hope you enjoy exploring or revisiting these patterns as much as I did. I found a new favorite or two while working on this book, and I hope you do too. Sure, styles have changed, yarns have been discontinued, and we've been through a lot. But we've done it all together, finding comfort in our stitches when we can. I hope that this book brings you more comfort and happiness in the years to come.

And so, I bring you 35 patterns spanning five of my books. Enjoy, and happy knitting.

—Jen *(she/her)*

# Supplies & Tools

In this book, there are certain supplies and tools that are used over and over again. Here are the supplies and tools I use when knitting shawls.

## KNITTING NEEDLES

The shawls in this book call for circular needles. If you're new to shawl knitting, you may be asking yourself why you need a circular needle when we're knitting flat, back and forth in rows. The reason is simple: shawls tend to have a lot of stitches on the needle at one time. Many shawls have over 300 or 400 stitches and beyond. That number of stitches simply won't fit on a traditional knitting needles. Additionally, using a circular needle allows some of the weight of the fabric to be held by the cord, which makes the knitting easier on your wrists.

The length of the circular needle as well as the type (aluminum, plastic, wood, etc.) really is personal preference. A 24" (61cm) circular needle is the shortest length you'll want to use. Even at that length, the stitches can get pretty crammed on the needles. I prefer a 32" (81.3cm) circular needle for my shawl knitting, in most cases.

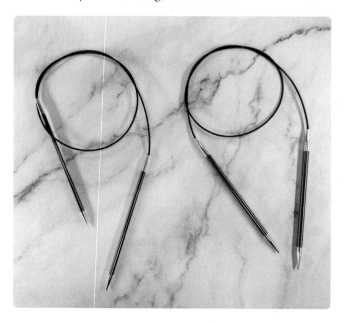

## STITCH MARKERS

Stitch markers are used in projects for a variety of reasons. You may need to mark a specific stitch or simply mark the right side or wrong side of your project. In many knitting patterns, you'll often need to section off the stitches on the knitting needle with stitch markers, whether it's to work a specific stitch pattern in between the stitch markers or to work shaping near the markers on the needle.

I prefer to use plastic locking stitch markers, but you should use whatever stitch markers you like best!

## SCISSORS

When your knitting project is complete, you'll need to cut the yarn with scissors to leave a yarn tail to weave in on your piece. There are so many different  types of scissors and cutting tools you can use. I personally love little folding travel scissors. They are lightweight and small enough that you can easily toss it into your project bag.

## TAPESTRY NEEDLES

Tapestry needles (also known as yarn needles or darning needles) are a necessary notion for completing your project. While these needles are often used simply to weave in the ends on a project, you can also use them for things like adding embroidery to a piece.

When choosing a tapestry needle, make sure the eye of the needle isn't too big. You want to make sure the needle can work in and out of your stitches smoothly; you don't want the eye to be so large that it stretches your stitches. Many tapestry needles are sold in packs, and often one pack will contain a variety of needles.

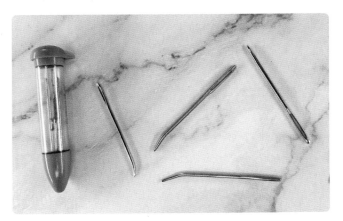

## BLOCKING SUPPLIES

What blocking supplies you want to use for your project depends on personal preference, the amount of space you have for blocking, and the fiber content in the shawl you have just completed.

If you are wet blocking your shawl (page 15), you'll need to start with some wool wash and a tub or bowl to place your shawl in. I have an old plastic chip bowl that I use for blocking most of my shawls. You can also fill a clean sink or bathtub. The type of wool wash you use is up to you—I prefer a no-rinse wool wash. You'll also need an old towel or two to soak up the excess water in the shawl. When blocking the shawl, I like to use a blocking mat with rust-proof pins or needles to shape my shawl.

If your shawl was knit out of a synthetic yarn, like acrylic, you'll need to steam block your shawl. In that case, you'll simply need an iron or other clothes-steaming device. **Remember:** Never touch an iron to your knitting, especially acrylic—it will melt!

Towel

Blocking combs

Blocking mat

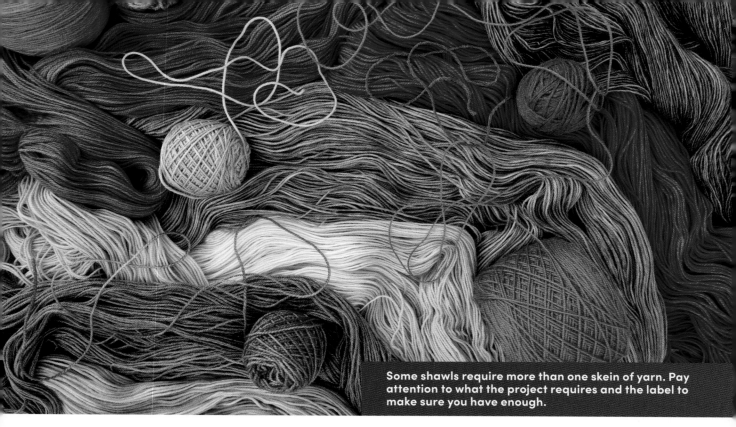

Some shawls require more than one skein of yarn. Pay attention to what the project requires and the label to make sure you have enough.

# Choosing the Right Yarn

Because this is a compilation of patterns from my previous books, sadly some of the yarn has been discontinued at the time of publication. Some companies have simply changed yarn bases over the years or perhaps some of the companies no longer sell yarn. Fortunately, there is no shortage of beautiful yarn for you to use for any of these projects!

There are many factors to take into consideration when picking out the right yarn for your project. Yardage is probably the most important consideration. Lots of yarn is hand dyed, so it may be impossible to get another matching skein later if you run out. So, just like with any project, make sure you check those yarn labels.

Color is also something to think about when picking yarn for your accessories. Multicolored yarn is beautiful, but sometimes, with a large, complicated stitch pattern, the yarn and stitches fight each other rather than work together to form a beautiful, finished piece.

For larger projects that use one yarn color, you'll want to consider alternating skeins of yarn for the duration of the project, especially if you are using hand-dyed yarn. Even when yarn skeins are dyed at the same time and have the same dye lot, they don't always match perfectly. To ensure your project looks one color throughout, switch skeins every two rows. Rather than switching skeins when you run out (causing a noticeable color difference), this method allows the slight differences in skeins to blend subtly.

Finally, fiber content is a very important consideration for choosing the right yarn. Many yarns contain at least some wool. My go-to yarns for accessory projects are ones that contain superwash merino. These items are going on someone's neck, head, hands, etc., and for many people, wool yarns that aren't superwash can be a little itchy, especially in those sensitive areas. But what if the recipient is sensitive or allergic to wool or other animal fibers? Fortunately, there are lots of yarns out there that don't contain any animal fibers at all. For shawl projects, I tend to avoid yarn that's 100% cotton because it can be hard to block and doesn't hold its shape well over time. But you can find yarn blends that contain bamboo, TENCEL™, nylon, silk, and more.

**From left to right: DK, worsted, and bulky yarn.**

**From left to right: DK, worsted, and bulky swatches.**

## YARN WEIGHT & SUBSTITUTIONS

One question I frequently receive from knitters concerns yarn weight and substitutions. When it comes to accessories, like scarves and shawls, that don't need to have a specific fit, it's usually pretty easy to switch to a thinner or thicker yarn, depending on your preference. It will change the finished size of the piece, but that isn't as critical as with projects that need to really fit, like mittens or a hat. But how exactly does changing the yarn weight affect the size of the finished item? To get a better understanding, let's compare DK-weight, worsted-weight, and bulky-weight yarns.

I used each of these yarns and knit a swatch. For each swatch, I used a needle within the recommended needle range given on the ball band for the yarn. All three swatches were worked as follows:

CO 25 sts. Knit 3 rows.
**Row 1 (RS):** Knit all sts.
**Row 2 (WS):** K2, purl to last 2 sts, K2.
Rep Rows 1 and 2 for a total of 28 rows.
Knit 4 rows. BO kwise on RS.

You can easily see that the thicker the yarn, the larger the swatch. From looking at the swatches, it's clear that if we use a thicker yarn and needle than the pattern recommends, and then knit the pattern as written, the item will end up being larger than the measurements given in the pattern.

That's good information to have, but the next consideration is this: Did we use more yarn on the bulky swatch? Yes! How do we know? Math! Let's compare the DK-weight swatch to the bulky-weight swatch to get a handle on the yarn amount used.

The ball band on the DK-weight yarn states that it contains 225 yds (205.7m) and is 3.5oz (100g). I can calculate the yards or meters per gram as follows:

$$225 \text{ yards} \div 100 \text{ grams} = 2.25 \text{ yards per gram}$$

$$206 \text{ meters} \div 100 \text{ grams} = 2.06 \text{ meters per gram}$$

I knit my swatch and then weighed it. The DK-weight swatch weighed 10 grams. I now multiply the weight of the swatch (10 grams) by the yards or meters per gram result.

$$10 \text{ grams} \times 2.25 \text{ yards per gram} = 22.5 \text{ yards}$$

$$10 \text{ grams} \times 2.06 \text{ meters per gram} = 20.6 \text{ meters}$$

I know that I used 22.5 yds (20.6m) in my DK-weight swatch. Now we can repeat the process for the bulky swatch. The ball band on the bulky-weight yarn indicates that there are 165 yds (150.9m) in the skein for 3.5oz (100g). Using the first equation above, we can determine that bulky yarn has 1.65 yds (1.51m) per gram. My completed swatch weighs 20 grams.

Using the second equation, we can calculate that I used 33 yds (30.2m) for my bulky swatch. When working a pattern the same way for a DK-weight and bulky-weight yarn, the bulky yarn will use more yarn and result in a larger finished piece!

Play around and experiment with different yarn weights on some of the projects—there are lots of shawls, scarves, and cowls to try! Be on the lookout for tip boxes, where I'll tell you which patterns are easy to adapt to your yarn choice.

# Shawl Knitting Basics

Here are some basic techniques that you will find commonly used throughout this book and will help you successfully knit your projects.

## GARTER-TAB CAST ON

Several projects in this book begin with a garter-tab cast on. Refer to the pattern you're knitting for the specific number of stitches to cast on and how many rows are to be worked—we're looking at the classic example here. This cast on is typically worked as follows:

**1.** Cast on three stitches and knit six rows.

**2.** Rotate work clockwise 90 degrees, and pick up three stitches evenly along the left edge. Try to insert the needle into each of the three bumps on the edge of the tab.

**3.** Rotate work clockwise 90 degrees again, and pick up three stitches evenly from the cast-on edge (nine stitches total). Turn your work and continue with the pattern as written.

# KNITTED CAST ON

Use this cast on to add extra stitches to a shawl, typically when working a border. You may also want to use it for those bottom-up shawls that start with a lot of stitches on the needle.

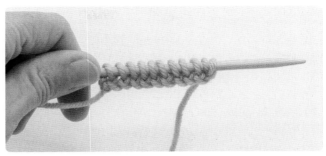

**1.** Start with a slipknot on the left-hand needle. Insert the right-hand needle into the slipknot as if to knit, yarn over, and pull a loop through. Transfer the new stitch from the right-hand needle to the left-hand needle.

**2.** Knit into the last stitch on the left-hand needle, and transfer the new stitch back to the left-hand needle until you have the correct number of stitches.

# CIRCULAR CAST ON

This is the cast on that is used for the Daylily Shawl (page 168)—it's perfect for circular shawls that are worked from the center outward. Once pulled tight, this cast on closes the hole at the center of the shawl.

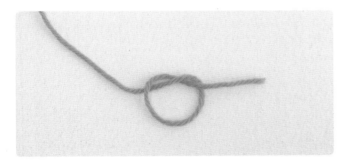

**1.** Cross the yarn over itself to make a loose knot. The tail will be on the right side and the working yarn on the left side.

**2.** With the working yarn in your left hand, use the right-hand needle to go into the knot, yarn over, and pull a loop through.

**3.** Yarn over above the hole to make your next stitch.

**4.** Repeat the last two steps, working into the knot and above the knot until you have the desired number of stitches. Once you start your shawl and work a few rounds, tug on the tail to pull the hole closed.

# REARRANGING STITCH MARKERS

When it comes to repeating a set of stitches across a row, some knitters find it helpful to place a stitch marker after each repeat. You can end up with a lot of stitch markers on the needle when you do this, but it can help you keep track of where you are in the pattern. However, placing a stitch marker at each lace repeat in the row can cause issues, depending on how the lace is set up. In some cases, you may have to "borrow a stitch" from the next repeat in order to complete the repeat you are working. This can become a little confusing, so let's look at an example.

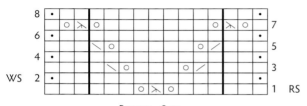

WS

Repeat = 9 sts

## Legend

| | | | |
|---|---|---|---|
| ☐ | K on RS, P on WS | ⟔ | Sk2p |
| · | P on RS, K on WS | \ | Ssk |
| ○ | YO | / | K2tog |

When working the chart to the left, you'll have to borrow a stitch from the next repeat when each repeat is split up with stitch markers.

Working the first row of the pattern, place the stitch markers at each repeat indicated by the bold vertical lines. When working the next five rows, just slip the markers along the way. When you get to Row 7, it will be time to borrow a stitch.

At the first double decrease, you will only have two stitches left before the marker, but you need three stitches in order to complete that stitch (bottom-left photo). Remove the stitch marker, complete the double-decrease stitch, and then place the stitch marker on the right needle (bottom-right photo).

Repeat this process across the row, moving the stitch marker at each repeat.

For patterns in this book where the stitch markers would need to be moved, you'll find details in the Pattern Notes for that particular project. Whether you decide to use lots of stitch markers or none at all is entirely up to you. If you do choose to add stitch markers at each repeat, hopefully this explanation of how to move them around when necessary will lead you to successful lace knitting.

**Three stitches are needed to complete the double decrease, but there are only two stitches before the marker.**

**The marker was removed, the stitch was completed, and the marker was placed back on the needle.**

## K2TOG TBL BIND OFF

You can bind off your project in a number of different ways. For a shawl, the goal is to have a bind off that's stretchy, so that when blocking the shawl, you can pull and form the edge any way you like.

The following is my favorite knitwise bind off. If you tend to bind off tightly, try using a needle one or two sizes larger than indicated

To work, knit the first two stitches together through the back loop. *Slip the stitch from the right needle to the left needle with the yarn in back and knit two together through the back loops; repeat from * until all stitches are bound off.

## BLOCKING

Soak the shawl in warm water, adding a wool wash if you like. After soaking 20 minutes or more, remove and ring it out with a towel. Use either blocking wires or pins to block it to the specified size.

For a triangular shawl, I like to run a wire along the top edge. Then carefully stretch it out, and pin the wires in place on a blocking board to dry. For the side edges, run a wire through the points you want to pull out. Then carefully stretch out the lace, and pin the wires in place.

For nontriangular shawls, either use a variety of wires at different angles or pin each point individually.

**Knit two stitches together through the back loops for a simple, stretchy bind off.**

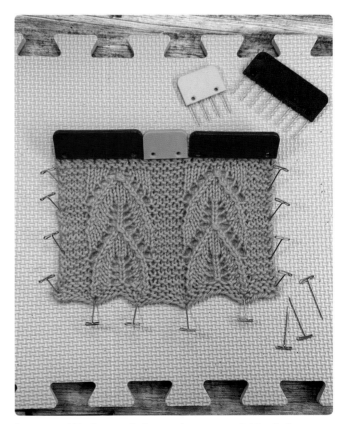

**Rustproof T-pins and pin combs are useful tools for blocking your projects.**

# Projects

Now that we know about the materials we need for our shawls, let's dive into the patterns. In the following pages, you'll find 35 beautiful shawl patterns, each with their own unique details that are a delight to knit. We'll explore lots of classic shawl shapes, with some fun challenges thrown in along the way. These are some of my absolute favorite shawls I've ever designed, and my hope is that you'll find a favorite or two (or three . . .) among them too.

If needed, refer to the Knitting Abbreviations (page 174) as you work through the instructions.

# Medley

There's something I love about simple ribbed scarves, but the unfortunate truth is that they can be a bit boring to knit. Not this scarf! Small cables are inserted between alternating rib patterns, making this scarf both fun to knit and cozy to wear.

## FINISHED MEASUREMENTS
- 9 1/2" × 70" (24.1 × 177.8cm)

## MATERIALS
- 492 yds (449.9m) DK-weight yarn
- US Size 7 (4.5mm) knitting needles, or size required for gauge
- Cable needle
- Tapestry needle
- Blocking supplies

## YARN INFORMATION
- Sample uses 4 skeins of City Tweed DK from Knit Picks (55% merino/25% superfine alpaca/20% Donegal tweed; 1.8oz/50g; 123 yds/112.5m) in color the Blue Blood

## GAUGE
- 18 sts and 28 rows = 4" (10.2cm) in (k2, p2) ribbing patt, blocked and slightly stretched
- *Gauge is not critical for this pattern; however, a different gauge will affect the finished size of the project as well as the amount of yarn needed.*

## PATTERN NOTES
- This scarf is worked primarily in a ribbed pattern. You may find it helpful to use a locking stitch marker to mark the right side of your project.

## SPECIAL ABBREVIATION
- **1/1 RC:** Sl1 to cable needle, hold in back, k1, k1 from cable needle.

**With the staggered ribbing and cables worked all the way across a row, even the reverse side of this project looks great. This photo shows the front of the scarf.**

## INSTRUCTIONS

CO 42 sts.

Using the chart or written instructions, work until scarf measures approximately 70" (177.8cm), ending with Row 8 or 18 of Chart.

### Written Instructions for Chart

*Depending on what you prefer, follow either the chart or the written instructions below.*

**Row 1 (RS):** *K2, p2; rep from * to last 2 sts, k2.

**Row 2 (WS):** P2, *K2, p2; rep from * to end.

**Rows 3–8:** Rep Rows 1 and 2 three times.

**Row 9:** *1/1 RC; rep from * to end.

**Row 10:** K2, *P2, k2; rep from * to end.

**Row 11:** *P2, k2; rep from * to last 2 sts, p2.

**Rows 12–17:** Rep Rows 10 and 11 three times.

**Row 18:** Rep Row 10.

**Row 19:** *1/1 RC; rep from * to end.

**Row 20:** Rep Row 2.

Rep Rows 1–20 for patt.

# Make It Your Own!

Medley is very easy to modify. You can change up the width of the scarf simply by casting on any multiple of 4, plus 2 stitches. Because the cast-on number is so easy to change, this is a great project to use a different yarn weight if you want. Use the appropriate needle for your yarn, decide how many stitches to cast on, and get knitting.

**Remember:** Changing the number of stitches or changing the yarn weight will affect the finished size as well as the amount of yarn needed to complete it.

# FINISHING

BO loosely kwise on RS. Block scarf to finished measurements given at beg of patt. With tapestry needle, weave in ends.

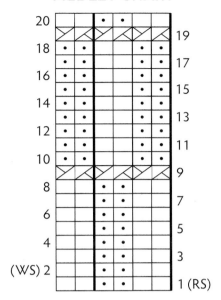

Repeat = 4 sts

## LEGEND

☐ K on RS, P on WS

⊡ P on RS, K on WS

⧄ 1/1 RC

# Adorn

Simple lace and stockinette stitch are the stars of this project. With extra increases added along the top edge, this triangle shawl will stay put on your shoulders, wrapping you like a warm hug.

## FINISHED MEASUREMENTS

- 56" wide × 18" deep (142.2 × 45.7cm)

## MATERIALS

- 400 yds (365.8m) DK-weight yarn
- US Size 5 (3.75mm) circular needle, 24" (61cm) cable or longer, or size required for gauge
- 2 stitch markers
- Tapestry needle
- Blocking supplies

## YARN INFORMATION

- Sample uses 1 skein of Artisan Sock from Hazel Knits (90% superwash merino/10% nylon; 4.2oz/120g; 400 yds/365.8m) in the color Sharkskin

## GAUGE

- 18 sts and 32 rows = 4" (10.2cm) in St st, blocked
- *Gauge is not critical for this pattern; however, a different gauge will affect the finished size of the project as well as the amount of yarn needed.*

**The small lace motif makes this pattern a great choice for multicolored yarn.**

## INSTRUCTIONS

Work garter-tab CO as follows:

CO 2 sts. Knit 18 rows. Turn work 90-degrees clockwise, and pick up and knit 9 sts along the left edge. Turn work 90-degrees clockwise, and pick up and knit 2 sts from CO edge—13 sts total.

**Set-Up Row 1 (WS):** K2, p9, k2.

**Set-Up Row 2 (RS):** K2, yo, k4, yo, pm, k1, pm, yo, k4, yo, k2—17 sts.

**Set-Up Row 3:** K3, yo, purl to last 3 sts, yo, K3—19 sts.

Using the chart or written instructions for the chart, work Chart twice—67 sts.

### Written Instructions for Chart

*Depending on what you prefer, follow either the chart or the written instructions below.*

**Row 1 (RS):** K2, yo, k2, *yo, k1, yo, sk2p; rep from * to 1 st before marker, k1, yo, sm, k1, sm, yo, k1, **sk2p, yo, k1, yo; rep from ** to last 4 sts, k2, yo, k2.

**Row 2 and all even-numbered rows (WS):** K3, yo, purl to last 3 sts, yo, k3.

**Row 3:** K2, yo, k4, *sk2p, yo, k1, yo; rep from * to 2 sts before marker, k2, yo, sm, k1, sm, yo, k2, **yo, k1, yo, sk2p; rep from ** to last 6 sts, k4, yo, k2.

**Row 5:** (K2, yo) twice, k1, yo, sk2p, *yo, k1, yo, sk2p; rep from * to 3 sts before marker, k3, yo, sm, k1, sm, yo, k3, **sk2p, yo, k1, yo; rep from ** to last 8 sts, sk2p, yo, k1, (yo, k2) twice.

**Row 7:** K2, yo, k4, *sk2p, yo, k1, yo; rep from * to 4 sts before marker, k4, yo, sm, k1, sm, yo, k4, **yo, k1, yo, sk2p; rep from ** to last 6 sts, k4, yo, k2.

**Row 8:** K3, yo, purl to last 3 sts, yo, k3.

Rep Rows 1–8 for patt.

# Make It Your Own!

With a second skein of yarn, you can add as many repeats of the chart as you like. You can also switch it up and alternate the chart and stockinette sections to add interest to your shawl. Just be sure to work the full eight rows of the stockinette section or chart before switching.

**Remember:** Changing the number of repeats you work or changing the yarn weight will affect the finished size of your shawl as well as the amount of yarn needed to complete it.

## STOCKINETTE STITCH SECTION

**Row 1 (RS):** K2, yo, knit to marker, yo, sm, k1, sm, yo, knit to last 2 sts, yo, k2—71 sts.

**Row 2 (WS):** k3, yo, purl to last 3 sts, yo, k3—73 sts. Rep Rows 1 and 2 another 3 times—91 sts.

## BODY OF SHAWL

Work Chart twice—139 sts.

Work Rows 1 and 2 of Stockinette Stitch section 4 times—163 sts.

Work Chart 6 times—307 sts.

## FINISHING

BO loosely kwise on RS. Block shawl to finished measurements given at beg of patt. With tapestry needle, weave in ends.

| STITCH COUNTS FOR SHAWL | |
|---|---|
| Following Set-Up Rows | 19 sts |
| Chart | 43 sts |
| Chart | 67 sts |
| Stockinette Stitch Section | 91 sts |
| Chart | 115 sts |
| Chart | 139 sts |
| Stockinette Stitch Section | 163 sts |
| Chart | 187 sts |
| Chart | 211 sts |
| Chart | 235 sts |
| Chart | 259 sts |
| Chart | 283 sts |
| Chart | 307 sts |

## ADORN CHART

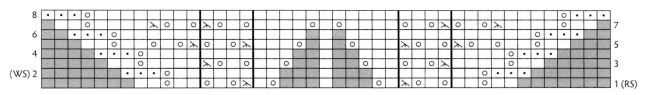

Repeat = 4 sts          Repeat = 4 sts

## LEGEND

- ☐ K on RS, P on WS
- • P on RS, K on WS
- ▨ No stitch
- ○ YO
- ⅄ Sk2p

# Inflorescence

This shawl flows from stockinette into a lacy floral pattern. Love the look of the lace at the edge of the shawl? With a second skein of yarn, you can make the lace section bigger and turn a flower bed into a whole garden!

## FINISHED MEASUREMENTS

- 60" wide × 26" deep (152.4 × 66cm)

## MATERIALS

- 435 yds (397.8m) fingering-weight yarn
- US Size 4 (3.5mm) circular needle, 32" (81.3cm) cable or longer, or size required for gauge
- 4 stitch markers
- Tapestry needle
- Blocking supplies

## YARN INFORMATION

- Sample uses 1 skein of Heritage from Cascade Yarns (75% superwash merino/25% nylon; 3.5oz/100g; 437 yds/399.6m) in color Cinnamon
- *The sample used almost the entire skein for the shawl. You may want to secure a second skein of yarn for your shawl.*

## GAUGE

- 20 sts and 32 rows = 4" (10.2cm) in St st, blocked
- *Gauge is not critical for this pattern; however, a different gauge will affect the finished size of the project as well as the amount of yarn needed.*

## PATTERN NOTES

- If using additional stitch markers to mark each stitch repeat, on some rows, the stitch markers will need to be rearranged. For this pattern, you'll need to rearrange these stitch markers on Row 7 of Chart C. For more information on this technique, see page 14.
- If you want to make your shawl a little smaller to ensure that you don't run out of yarn, work Rows 2 and 3 (under Instructions) 35 times total—153 sts. From there, you can continue the pattern as written, with one more Row 2 being worked, followed by the charts.

**The stockinette stitch body of the shawl flows easily into the lace pattern.**

## BODY OF SHAWL

Work garter-tab CO as follows:

CO 3 sts. Knit 6 rows. Turn work 90-degrees clockwise, and pick up and knit 3 sts along the left edge. Turn work 90-degrees clockwise, and pick up and knit 3 sts from CO edge—9 sts total.

**Row 1 (RS):** K3, pm, yo, k1, yo, pm, k1 (center st), pm, yo, k1, yo, pm, k3—13 sts.

**Row 2 (WS):** K3, purl to last 3 sts, k3.

**Row 3:** K3, sm, yo, knit to next marker, yo, sm, k1, sm, yo, knit to last 3 sts, yo, sm, k3.

Work Rows 2 and 3 another 52 times.

Work Row 2 once more—225 sts.

## LACE EDGING

Continue working first 3 sts and last 3 sts in garter st (knit every row), and center st in St st (knit on RS, purl on WS) and work charts as follows:

Using the chart or written instructions, work Chart A between st markers on each half of shawl—241 sts.

Using the chart or written instructions, work Chart B between st markers on each half of shawl—273 sts.

Using the chart or written instructions, work Chart C between st markers on each half of shawl—321 sts.

### Written Instructions for Chart A

*Depending on what you prefer, follow either the chart or the written instructions below.*

**Row 1 (RS):** Yo, k1, yo, ssk, k3, *k4, k2tog, yo, k1, yo, ssk, k3; rep from * to 7 sts before marker, k4, k2tog, yo, k1, yo.

**Row 2 and all even-numbered rows (WS):** Purl all sts.

**Row 3:** Yo, k3, yo, ssk, k2, *k3, k2tog, yo, k3, yo, ssk, k2; rep from * to 8 sts before marker, k3, k2tog, yo, k3, yo.

**Row 5:** Yo, k2tog, yo, k1, (yo, ssk) twice, k1, *k2, (k2tog, yo) twice, k1, (yo, ssk) twice, k1; rep from * to 9 sts before marker, k2, (k2tog, yo) twice, k1, yo, ssk, yo.

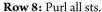

**Row 7:** Yo, k2tog, yo, k3, (yo, ssk) twice, *k1, (k2tog, yo) twice, k3, (yo, ssk) twice; rep from * to 10 sts before marker, k1, (k2tog, yo) twice, k3, yo, ssk, yo.

**Row 8:** Purl all sts.

# Make It Your Own!

If you have a second skein of yarn, repeat Chart A and Chart B one more time before moving on to Chart C to add some length to your shawl.

## Written Instructions for Chart B

*Depending on what you prefer, follow either the chart or the written instructions below.*

**Row 1 (RS):** Yo, k4, yo, k1, yo, k3, k2tog, *k1, ssk, k3, yo, k1, yo, k3, k2tog; rep from * to 11 sts before marker, k1, ssk, k3, yo, k1, yo, k4, yo.

**Row 2 and all even-numbered rows (WS):** Purl all sts.

**Row 3:** Yo, k5, yo, k3, yo, k2, k2tog, *k1, ssk, k2, yo, k3, yo, k2, k2tog; rep from * to 13 sts before marker, k1, ssk, k2, yo, k3, yo, k5, yo.

**Row 5:** Yo, k2, *(k1, yo, ssk) twice, (k1, k2tog, yo) twice; rep from * to 3 sts before marker, k3, yo.

**Row 7:** Yo, k3, *k2, yo, ssk, k1, yo, sk2p, yo, k1, k2tog, yo, k1; rep from * to 4 sts before marker, k4, yo.

**Row 9:** Yo, k2, k2tog, yo, *k1, (yo, ssk) twice, k3, (k2tog, yo) twice; rep from * to 5 sts before marker, k1, yo, ssk, k2, yo.

**Row 11:** Yo, k2, k2tog, yo, k1, *k2, (yo, ssk) twice, k1, (k2tog, yo) twice, k1; rep from * to 6 sts before marker, k2, yo, ssk, k2, yo.

**Row 12:** Purl all sts.

## Written Instructions for Chart C

*Depending on what you prefer, follow either the chart or the written instructions below.*

**Row 1 (RS):** Yo, k1, ssk, k3, yo, *k1, yo, k3, k2tog, k1, ssk, k3, yo; rep from * to 7 sts before marker, k1, yo, k3, k2tog, k1, yo.

**Row 2 and all even-numbered rows (WS):** Purl all sts.

**Row 3:** Yo, k2, ssk, k2, yo, k1, *k2, yo, k2, k2tog, k1, ssk, k2, yo, k1; rep from * to 8 sts before marker, k2, yo, k2, k2tog, k2, yo.

**Row 5:** Yo, k3, yo, ssk, k1, yo, ssk, *(k1, k2tog, yo) twice, (k1, yo, ssk) twice; rep from * to 9 sts before marker, (k1, k2tog, yo) twice, k3, yo.

**Row 7:** Yo, k5, yo, ssk, k1, yo, *sk2p, yo, k1, k2tog, yo, k3, yo, ssk, k1, yo; rep from * to 11 sts before marker, sk2p, yo, k1, k2tog, yo, k5, yo.

**Row 9:** Yo, (k2tog, yo) twice, k1, (yo, ssk) twice, k1, *k2, (k2tog, yo) twice, k1, (yo, ssk) twice, k1; rep from * to 11 sts before marker, k2, (k2tog, yo) twice, k1, (yo, ssk) twice, yo.

**Row 11:** Yo, (k2tog, yo) twice, k3, (yo, ssk) twice, *k1, (k2tog, yo) twice, k3, (yo, ssk) twice; rep from * to 12 sts before marker, k1, (k2tog, yo) twice, k3, (yo, ssk) twice, yo.

**Row 13:** Yo, *k1, ssk, k3, yo, k1, yo, k3, k2tog; rep from * to last st before marker, k1, yo.

**Row 15:** Yo, k1, *k1, ssk, k2, yo, k3, yo, k2, k2tog; rep from * to 2 sts before marker, k2, yo.

**Row 17:** Yo, k2tog, yo, *(k1, yo, ssk) twice, (k1, k2tog, yo) twice; rep from * to 3 sts before marker, k1, yo, ssk, yo.

**Row 19:** Yo, k2tog, yo, k1, *k2, yo, ssk, k1, yo, sk2p, yo, k1, k2tog, yo, k1; rep from * to 4 sts before marker, k2, yo, ssk, yo.

**Row 21:** Yo, (k2tog, yo) twice, *k1, (yo, ssk) twice, k3, (k2tog, yo) twice; rep from * to 5 sts before marker, k1, (yo, ssk) twice, yo.

**Row 23:** Yo, (k2tog, yo) twice, k1, *k2, (yo, ssk) twice, k1, (k2tog, yo) twice, k1; rep from * to 6 sts before marker, k2, (yo, ssk) twice, yo.

## FINISHING

BO loosely kwise on WS. Block shawl to finished measurements given at beg of patt. With tapestry needle, weave in ends.

## INFLORESCENCE CHART A

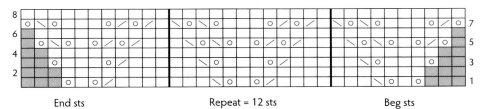

End sts          Repeat = 12 sts          Beg sts

## INFLORESCENCE CHART B

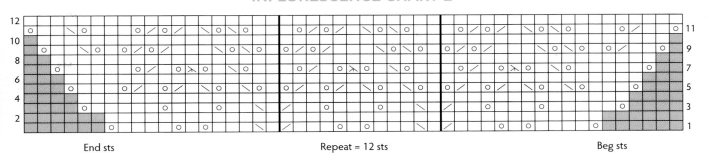

End sts          Repeat = 12 sts          Beg sts

## INFLORESCENCE CHART C

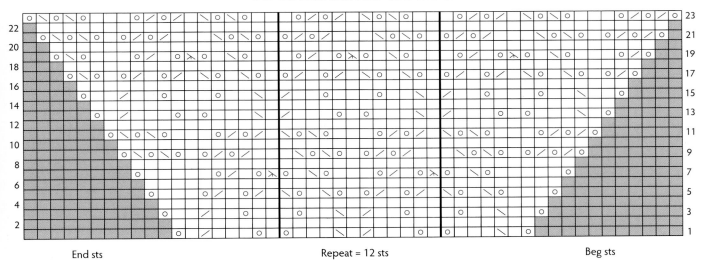

End sts          Repeat = 12 sts          Beg sts

## LEGEND

| | | | |
|---|---|---|---|
| ⊙ | YO | ╱ | K2tog |
| ☐ | K on RS, P on WS | ⋌ | SK2P |
| ╲ | Ssk | ▨ | No stitch |

# Juniper

The Juniper shawl is crescent shaped, knit from the lace edge, and worked upward to the neck edge. Short rows in the stockinette body of the shawl create a curved shape.

## FINISHED MEASUREMENTS

- 46" wide × 12" deep (116.8 × 30.5cm)

## MATERIALS

- 420 yds (384m) fingering-weight yarn
- US Size 5 (3.75mm) circular needle, 24" (61cm) cable or longer, or size required for gauge
- Tapestry needle
- Blocking supplies

## YARN INFORMATION

- Sample uses 1 skein of BFL Sock from Huckleberry Knits (80% merino/20% nylon; 3.5oz/100g; 420 yds/384m) in color Garnet

## GAUGE

- 18 sts and 32 rows = 4" (10.2cm) in St st, blocked
- *Gauge is not critical for this pattern; however, a different gauge will affect the finished size of the project as well as the amount of yarn needed.*

**The V-shaped lace pattern creates a beautiful scalloped edge on the shawl.**

# BODY OF SHAWL

CO 349 sts.

Knit 2 rows.

Using the chart or written instructions, work Chart A 3 times.

Using the chart or written instructions, work Chart B once—273 sts.

## Written Instructions for Chart A

*Depending on what you prefer, follow either the chart or the written instructions below.*

**Row 1 (RS):** K2, p1, *k1tbl, p1, k2tog, k1, yo, k1, k2tog, (k1, yo) twice, k1, ssk, k1, yo, k1, ssk, p1; rep from * to last 4 sts, k1tbl, p1, k2.

**Row 2 (WS):** K3, p1tbl, *k1, p15, k1, p1tbl; rep from * to last 3 sts, k3.

**Row 3:** K2, p1, *k1tbl, p1, yo, ssk, k1, k2tog, k1, yo, k3, yo, k1, ssk, k1, k2tog, yo, p1; rep from * to last 4 sts, k1tbl, p1, k2.

**Row 4:** K3, p1tbl, *k2, p13, k2, p1tbl; rep from * to last 3 sts, k3.

**Row 5:** K2, p1, *k1tbl, p2, yo, sk2p, k1, yo, k5, yo, k1, sk2p, yo, p2; rep from * to last 4 sts, k1tbl, p1, k2.

**Row 6:** K3, p1tbl, *k2, p13, k2, p1tbl; rep from * to last 3 sts, k3.

**Row 7:** K2, p1, *k1tbl, p2, k2tog, k1, yo, k7, yo, k1, ssk, p2; rep from * to last 4 sts, k1tbl, p1, k2.

**Row 8:** K3, p1tbl, *k2, p13, k2, p1tbl; rep from * to last 3 sts, k3.

## Written Instructions for Chart B

*Depending on what you prefer, follow either the chart or the written instructions below.*

**Row 1 (RS):** K2, p1, *k1tbl, p1, k2tog, k1, yo, k1, k2tog, (k1, yo) twice, k1, ssk, k1, yo, k1, ssk, p1; rep from * to last 4 sts, k1tbl, p1, k2.

**Row 2 (WS):** K3, p1tbl, *k1, p15, k1, p1tbl; rep from * to last 3 sts, k3.

**Row 3:** K2, p1, *k1tbl, p1, yo, ssk, k1, k2tog, k1, yo, k3, yo, k1, ssk, k1, k2tog, yo, p1; rep from * to last 4 sts, k1tbl, p1, k2.

**Row 4:** K3, p1tbl, *k1, p15, k1, p1tbl; rep from * to last 3 sts, k3.

**Row 5:** K2, p1, *k1tbl, p1, k1, sk2p, k1, yo, k5, yo, k1, sk2p, k1, p1; rep from * to last 4 sts, k1tbl, p1, k2.

**Row 6:** K3, p1tbl, *k1, p13, k1, p1tbl; rep from * to last 3 sts, k3.

**Row 7:** K2, p1, *k1tbl, p1, k2tog, k1, yo, k1, k2tog, k1, ssk, k1, yo, k1, ssk, p1; rep from * to last 4 sts, k1tbl, p1, k2.

**Row 8:** K3, p1tbl, *k1, p11, k1, p1tbl; rep from * to last 3 sts, k3.

## SHORT-ROW SECTION 1

**Row 1 (RS):** K141, turn work—132 sts unworked.

**Row 2 (WS):** P9, turn work—132 sts unworked.

**Row 3:** K8, ssk, k3, turn work—128 sts unworked; 272 sts total.

**Row 4:** P11, p2tog, p3, turn work—128 sts unworked; 271 sts total.

**Row 5:** Knit to 1 st before gap (1 st before previous turning point), ssk, k3, turn work.

**Row 6:** Purl to 1 st before gap (1 st before previous turning point), p2tog, p3, turn work.

Work Rows 5 and 6 another 15 times—64 sts unworked on each end of shawl; 239 sts total.

## SHORT-ROW SECTION 2

**Row 1 (RS):** Knit to 1 st before gap (1 st before previous turning point), ssk, k7, turn work.

**Row 2 (WS):** Purl to 1 st before gap (1 st before previous turning point), p2tog, p7, turn work.

Work Rows 1 and 2 another 6 times—8 sts unworked on each end of shawl; 225 sts total.

**Rows 3 and 4:** Knit to 1 st before gap (1 st before previous turning point), ssk, k7, turn work. All sts have been worked—223 sts.

## FINISHING

BO loosely kwise on RS Block shawl to finished measurements given at beg of patt. With tapestry needle, weave in ends.

### JUNIPER CHART A

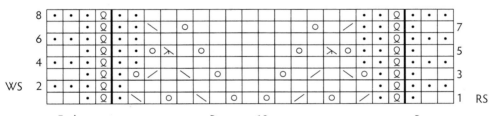

End sts    Repeat = 18 sts    Beg sts

### JUNIPER CHART B

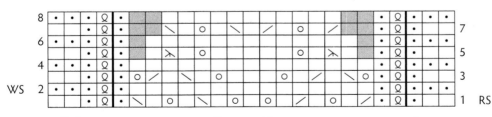

End sts    Repeat = 18 sts    Beg sts
(decreases to 16 sts on row 5 and to 14 sts on row 7)

### LEGEND

| | |
|---|---|
| ☐ K on RS, P on WS | ☐ YO |
| ⦁ P on RS, K on WS | ⟍ Ssk |
| Ω K1tbl on RS, P1tbl on WS | ⋊ Sk2p |
| ⁄ K2tog | ▨ No stitch |

# Damsel

A lace pattern used two ways makes for an interesting project. This shawl is worked from the top down using an allover lace pattern; a knitted-on border is added at the end using the same motif with a slight variation.

## FINISHED MEASUREMENTS

- 70" wide × 23" deep (177.8 × 58.4cm)

## MATERIALS

- 675 yds (617.2m) DK-weight yarn
- US Size 6 (4.0mm) circular needle, 32" (81.3cm) cable or longer, or size required for gauge
- Tapestry needle
- Blocking supplies

## YARN INFORMATION

- Sample uses 3 skeins of Tosh DK from Madelinetosh (100% superwash merino wool; 3.5oz/100g; 225 yds/205.7m) in the color Gossamer

## GAUGE

- 20 sts and 28 rows = 4" (10.2cm) in St st, blocked
- *Gauge is not critical for this pattern; however, a different gauge will affect the finished size of the project as well as the amount of yarn needed.*

## PATTERN NOTES

- If using stitch markers to mark each stitch repeat, on some rows, the stitch markers will need to be rearranged. For this pattern, you'll need to rearrange these stitch markers on Rows 3 and 7 of Chart A. For more information on this technique, see page 14.
- For Chart B, the final ssk on RS rows is worked by using last st from border and first st on LH needle from body of shawl.
- On Row 7 of Chart B, after binding off 3 sts, there is 1 st on RH needle. This counts as the first st worked after the stitches are bound off (i.e., it's the first st of the k4 that follows the binding off).

**The body of this shawl contains an allover stitch pattern. The same stitch is slightly modified and used in the lace border edging.**

## INSTRUCTIONS

Work garter-tab CO as follows:
CO 2 sts. Knit 22 rows. Turn work
90-degrees clockwise, and pick up
and knit 11 sts along the left edge.
Turn work 90-degrees clockwise,
and pick up and knit 2 sts from CO
edge—15 sts total.

**Set-Up Row (WS):** K2, p11, k2.
**Inc Row (RS):** K2, (yo, k1) to last 2
sts, yo, k2—27 sts.
**Next Row:** K2, purl to last 2 sts, k2.

## BODY OF SHAWL

Using the chart or written
instructions, work Chart A 11
times total.
Work Rows 1–7 of Chart A
once more.
**Next Row (WS):** K2, yo, (k1, kfb) twice, knit to the last 4 sts, kfb, k1, yo, k2—318 sts.

| STITCH COUNT FOR BODY OF SHAWL | |
|---|---|
| Rep 1 of Chart A | 51 sts |
| Rep 2 of Chart A | 75 sts |
| Rep 3 of Chart A | 99 sts |
| Rep 4 of Chart A | 123 sts |
| Rep 5 of Chart A | 147 sts |
| Rep 6 of Chart A | 171 sts |
| Rep 7 of Chart A | 195 sts |
| Rep 8 of Chart A | 219 sts |
| Rep 9 of Chart A | 243 sts |
| Rep 10 of Chart A | 267 sts |
| Rep 11 of Chart A | 291 sts |
| Rows 1–7 only of Chart A | 313 sts |

### Written Instructions for Chart A

*Depending on what you prefer, follow either the chart or the written instructions below.*
**Row 1 (RS):** K2, (yo, k1) twice, *k2tog, (k1, yo) twice, k1, ssk, k5; rep from * to last 11 sts, k2tog, (k1, yo) twice, k1, ssk, (k1, yo) twice, k2.
**Row 2 and all even-numbered rows (WS):** K2, yo, k1, purl to the last 3 sts, k1, yo, k2.
**Row 3:** K2, yo, k1, yo, k3, k2tog, *k1, yo, k3, yo, k1, sssk, (k1, yo, k1) into next st, k3tog; rep from * to last 13 sts, k1, yo, k3, yo, k1, ssk, k3, yo, k1, yo, k2.

# Make It Your Own!

It's easy to adjust the size of this shawl, making it a great project for substituting yarn weights. Work Chart A to the desired length, and then work Rows 1–7 of Chart A once more.
 Finish the body of the shawl by working the final WS row. Work the lace border section as written, adjusting the number of times Chart B is worked as necessary. Remember, changing the number of repeats you work or changing the yarn weight will affect the finished size of your shawl as well as the amount of yarn needed to complete it.

**Row 5:** K2, (yo, k1) twice, k2tog, (k1, yo) twice, k1, *ssk, k5, k2tog, (k1, yo) twice, k1; rep from * to last 6 sts, ssk, (k1, yo) twice, k2.

**Row 7:** K2, yo, k1, yo, k3, k2tog, k1, yo, k3, yo, *k1, sssk, (k1, yo, k1) into next st, k3tog, k1, yo, k3, yo; rep from * to last 9 sts, k1, ssk, k3, yo, k1, yo, k2.

**Row 8:** K2, yo, k1, purl to the last 3 sts, k1, yo, k2.

Rep Rows 1–8 for patt.

## LACE EDGING

With RS facing and using the knitted cast on, CO 17 sts.

**Next Row (RS):** K16, ssk with 1 st from body of shawl, turn.

**Next Row (WS):** Sl1 wyib, knit to end, turn.

Using the chart or written instructions, work Chart B 79 times.

**Next Row (RS):** K16, ssk with 1 st from body of shawl, turn.

**Next Row (WS):** Sl1 wyib, knit to end, turn.

### Written Instructions for Chart B

*Depending on what you prefer, follow either the chart or the written instructions below.*

**Row 1 (RS):** K2, yo, k2tog, yo, k1, k2tog, (k1, yo) twice, k1, ssk, k4, ssk the last border st with the first body st on left needle, turn.

**Row 2 and all even-numbered rows (WS):** Sl1 wyib, k1, purl to the last 2 sts, k2, turn.

**Row 3:** K2, yo, k2tog, yo, k1, k2tog, k1, yo, k3, yo, k1, ssk, k3, ssk the last border st with the first body st on left needle, turn.

**Row 5:** K2, yo, k2tog, (yo, k1) twice, ssk, k5, k2tog, k1, yo, k2, ssk the last border st with the first body st on left needle, turn.

**Row 7:** BO 3 sts, k4, yo, k1, sssk, (k1, yo, k1) into next st, k3tog, k1, yo, k3, ssk the last border st with the first body st on left needle, turn.

**Row 8:** Sl1 wyib, k1, purl to the last 2 sts, k2, turn.

Rep Rows 1–8 for patt.

## FINISHING

BO loosely kwise on RS. Block shawl to finished measurements given at beg of patt. With tapestry needle, weave in ends.

### DAMSEL CHART B

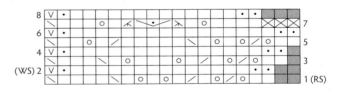

### LEGEND

| | |
|---|---|
| ☐ K on RS, P on WS | ⬈ K3tog on RS |
| • P on RS, K on WS | ⬊ Sssk on RS |
| ○ YO | ⟋⟍ (K1, YO, K1) into same st |
| ⟋ K2tog on RS | V Sl st pw wyib on WS |
| ⟍ Ssk on RS | ▨ No stitch |

### DAMSEL CHART A

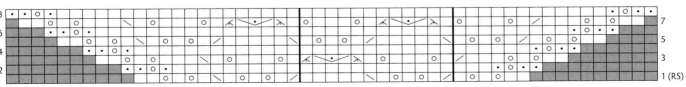

Repeat = 12 sts

# Ladybug

Use your imagination and look closely at the lace. Could there be ladybugs climbing along the edge of this pretty, airy shawlette?

## FINISHED MEASUREMENTS
- 50" wide × 21" deep (127 × 53.3cm)

## MATERIALS
- 420 yds (384m) fingering-weight yarn
- US Size 4 (3.5mm) circular needle, 32" (81.3cm) cable or longer, or size required for gauge
- 4 stitch markers
- Tapestry needle
- Blocking supplies

## YARN INFORMATION
- Sample uses 1 skein of Foot Notes from Fiber Optic Yarns (80% superwash merino wool/20% nylon; 4oz/114g; 420 yds/384m) in color Batik

## GAUGE
- 20 sts and 34 rows = 4" (10.2cm) in St st, blocked
- *Gauge is not critical for this pattern; however, a different gauge will affect the finished size of the project as well as the amount of yarn needed.*

## PATTERN NOTES
- If using additional stitch markers to mark each stitch repeat, on some rows, the stitch markers will need to be rearranged. For this pattern, you'll need to rearrange these stitch markers on Rows 7 and 9 of Chart C. For more information on this technique, see page 14.

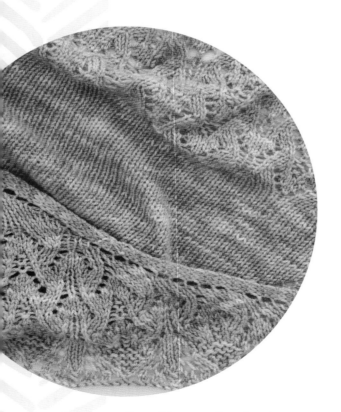

**One of the very first shawls I designed for my very first book, the lovely lace of Ladybug is still one of my favorites today.**

## BODY OF SHAWL

Work garter-tab CO as follows:

CO 3 sts. Knit 6 rows. Turn work 90-degrees clockwise, and pick up and knit 3 sts along the left edge. Turn work 90-degrees clockwise, and pick up and knit 3 sts from CO edge—9 sts total.

**Row 1 (RS):** K3, pm, yo, k1, yo, pm, k1 (center st), pm, yo, k1, yo, pm, k3—13 sts.

**Row 2 (WS):** K3, purl to last 3 sts, k3.

**Row 3:** K3, sm, yo, knit to next marker, yo, sm, k1, sm, yo, knit to last 3 sts, yo, sm, k3.

Work Rows 2 and 3 another 34 times—153 sts.

Rep Row 2 once more.

## LACE EDGING

Continue working first 3 sts and last 3 sts in garter st (knit every row), and center st in St st (knit on RS, purl on WS) and work charts as follows:

Using the chart or written instructions, work Chart A between st markers on each half of shawl 3 times—297 sts.

Using the chart or written instructions, work Chart B between st markers on each half of shawl—333 sts.

### Written Instructions for Chart A

*Depending on what you prefer, follow either the chart or the written instructions below.*

**Row 1 (RS):** Yo, k1, *ssk, k3, yo, k1, yo, k3, k2tog, k1; rep from * to marker, yo.

**Row 2 and all even-numbered rows (WS):** Purl all sts.

**Row 3:** Yo, k2, *ssk, k2, yo, k3, yo, k2, k2tog, k1; rep from * to 1 st before marker, k1, yo.

**Row 5:** Yo, k3, *ssk, k1, yo, k5, yo, k1, k2tog, k1; rep from * to 2 sts before marker, k2, yo.

**Row 7:** Yo, k3, yo, k1, *yo, k3, k2tog, p1, ssk, k3, yo, k1; rep from * to 3 sts before marker, yo, k3, yo.

**Row 9:** (Yo, k2) 3 times, *k1, yo, k2, k2tog, p1, ssk, k2, yo, k2; rep from * to 5 sts before marker, k1, yo, (k2, yo) twice.

| STITCH COUNTS FOR CHART A REPEATS | |
|---|---|
| First rep of Chart A | 201 sts |
| Second rep of Chart A | 249 sts |
| Third rep of Chart A | 297 sts |

# Make It Bigger!

With extra yarn, you can continue working Chart A as many times as you like before moving on to Chart B.

**Row 11:** (Yo, k2) 3 times, yo, k3, *k2, yo, k1, k2tog, p1, ssk, k1, yo, k3; rep from * to 8 sts before marker, (k2, yo) 4 times.

**Row 12:** Purl all sts.

Rep Rows 1–12 for patt.

## Written Instructions for Chart B

*Depending on what you prefer, follow either the chart or the written instructions below.*

**Row 1 (RS):** Yo, k1, *k1, yo, k1, k2tog, p3, ssk, k1, yo, k2; rep from * to marker, yo.

**Row 2 and all even-numbered rows (WS):** Purl all sts.

**Row 3:** (Yo, k1) twice, *k1, yo, k2tog, p5, ssk, yo, k2; rep from * to 1 st before marker, yo, k1, yo.

**Row 5:** (Yo, k2) twice, *k1, yo, k1, ssk, p3, k2tog, k1, yo, k2; rep from * to 3 sts before marker, k1, yo, k2, yo.

**Row 7:** Yo, k1, yo, k2tog, yo, k1, yo, sk2p, *(yo, k1) twice, ssk, p1, k2tog, (k1, yo) twice, sk2p; rep from * to 4 sts before marker, yo, k1, yo, ssk, yo, k1, yo.

**Row 9:** Yo, k2, yo, k2tog, (yo, k1) twice, sk2p, *(k1, yo) twice, k1, sk2p; rep from * to 6 sts before marker, (k1, yo) twice, ssk, yo, k2, yo.

## FINISHING

BO loosely kwise on WS. Block shawl to finished measurements given at beg of patt. With tapestry needle, weave in ends.

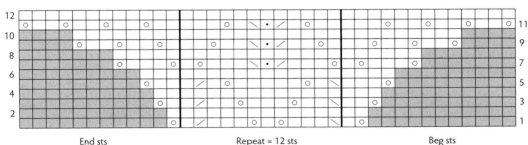

LADYBUG CHART A

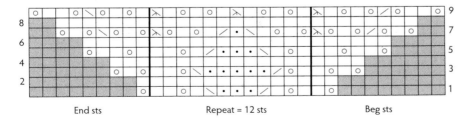

LADYBUG CHART B

LEGEND

# Starlit

This bottom-up short-row shawl features treelike lace at the edge that flows into the stockinette-stitch body. Try this shawl in a gradient yarn, and it just might look like the northern lights bouncing off the night sky.

## FINISHED MEASUREMENTS
- 78" wide × 17" deep (198.1 × 43.2cm)

## MATERIALS
- 660 yds (603.5m) fingering-weight yarn
- US Size 4 (3.5mm) circular needle, 32" (81.3cm) cable or longer, or size required for gauge
- Tapestry needle
- Blocking supplies

## YARN INFORMATION
- Sample uses 2 skeins of Muse from Twisted Fiber Art (50% silk/50% merino; 2.5oz/70g; 330 yds/301.8m) in color Phantom

## GAUGE
- 16 sts and 36 rows = 4" (10.2cm) in St st, blocked
- *Gauge is not critical for this pattern; however, a different gauge will affect the finished size of the project as well as the amount of yarn needed.*

## PATTERN NOTES
- If using stitch markers to mark each stitch repeat, on some rows, the stitch markers will need to be rearranged. For this pattern, you'll need to rearrange these markers on Row 5 of Chart A, and on Rows 9, 11, 13, and 15 of Chart B. For more information on this technique, see page 14.

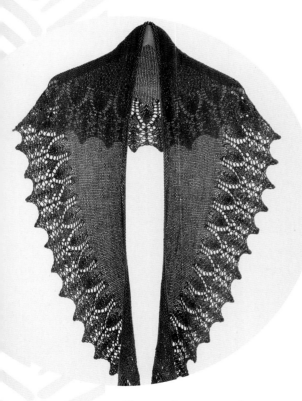

**The gradient yarn adds extra dimension to the lace edge.**

## INSTRUCTIONS

CO 435 sts.

Using the chart or written instructions, work Chart A 3 times.

Using the chart or written instructions, work Chart B—349 sts.

### Written Instructions for Chart A

*Depending on what you prefer, follow either the chart or the written instructions below.*

**Row 1 (RS):** K2, k2tog, k3, yo, k1, *yo, k3, sk2p, k3, yo, k1; rep from * to last 7 sts, yo, k3, ssk, k2.

**Row 2 (WS):** K2, purl to last 2 sts, k2.

**Row 3:** K2, k2tog, k2, yo, k2, *k1, yo, k2, sk2p, k2, yo, k2; rep from * to last 7 sts, k1, yo, k2, ssk, k2.

**Row 4:** K2, purl to last 2 sts, k2.

**Row 5:** K2, k2tog, (k1, yo) twice, sk2p, *(yo, k1) twice, sk2p, (k1, yo) twice, sk2p; rep from * to last 6 sts, (yo, k1) twice, ssk, k2.

**Row 6:** K2, purl to last 2 sts, k2.

### Written Instructions for Chart B

*Depending on what you prefer, follow either the chart or the written instructions below.*

**Row 1 (RS):** K2, *k3, k2tog, yo, k1, yo, ssk, k2; rep from * to last 3 sts, k3.

**Row 2 and all even-numbered rows (WS):** K2, purl to last 2 sts, k2.

**Row 3:** K2, *k2, k2tog, yo, k3, yo, ssk, k1; rep from * to last 3 sts, k3.

**Row 5:** K2, *k1, k2tog, yo, k5, yo, ssk; rep from * to last 3 sts, k3.

**Row 7:** K2, k2tog, yo, k4, *k3, yo, sk2p, yo, k4; rep from * to last 7 sts, k3, yo, ssk, k2.

**Row 9:** K2, *k1, yo, k3, sk2p, k3, yo; rep from * to last 3 sts, k3.

**Rows 11 and 13:** Rep Row 9.

**Row 15:** K2, *k1, yo, ssk, k1, sk2p, k1, k2tog, yo; rep from * to last 3 sts, k3.

**Row 16:** K2, purl to last 2 sts, k2.

# Make It Bigger!

Have more yarn? Repeat Chart A as many times as you like before moving on to Chart B.

## SHORT-ROW SECTION

**Row 1 (RS):** K179, turn work—170 sts unworked.

**Row 2 (WS):** P9, turn work—170 sts unworked.

**Row 3:** K8, ssk, k4, turn work—165 sts unworked; 348 sts total.

**Row 4:** P12, p2tog, p4, turn work—165 sts unworked; 347 sts total.

**Row 5:** Knit to 1 st before gap (1 st before previous turning point), ssk, k4, turn work.

**Row 6:** Purl to 1 st before gap (1 st before previous turning point), p2tog, p4, turn work.

Rep Rows 5 and 6 another 32 times—all sts have been worked; 281 sts rem.

Knit 4 rows.

## FINISHING

BO loosely kwise on RS. Block shawl to finished measurements given at beg of patt. With tapestry needle, weave in ends.

### STARLIT CHART A

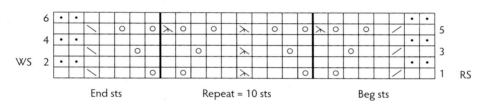

End sts      Repeat = 10 sts      Beg sts

### STARLIT CHART B

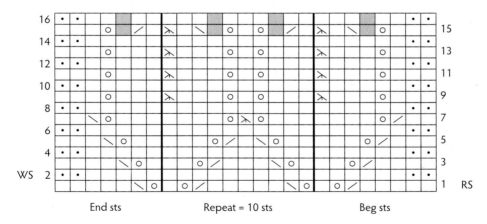

End sts      Repeat = 10 sts      Beg sts

### LEGEND

| | | | |
|---|---|---|---|
| ☐ | K on RS, P on WS | ╱ | K2tog |
| • | P on RS, K on WS | ⋋ | Sk2p |
| ╲ | Ssk | ▨ | No stitch |
| ○ | YO | | |

# Cheyenne

I can't help myself—I love combining garter stitch and lace. Cheyenne uses simple triangle-lace patterns broken up by rows of garter stitch with semicircular shaping.

## FINISHED MEASUREMENTS
- 54" wide × 26" deep (137.2 × 66cm)

## MATERIALS
- 750 yds (685.8m) DK-weight yarn
- US Size 6 (4.0mm) circular needle, 32" (81.3cm) cable or longer, or size required for gauge
- Tapestry needle
- Blocking supplies

## YARN INFORMATION
- Sample uses 3 skeins of Cricket from Anzula Luxury Fibers (80% superwash merino/10% cashmere/10% nylon; 3.5oz/100g; 250 yds/228.6m) in the color Coco

## GAUGE
- 20 sts and 28 rows = 4" (10.2cm) in St st, blocked
- *Gauge is not critical for this pattern; however, a different gauge will affect the finished size of the project as well as the amount of yarn needed.*

**The body of this shawl contains an allover stitch pattern. The same stitch is slightly modified and used in the lace border edging.**

## INSTRUCTIONS

Work garter-tab CO as follows:

CO 2 sts. Knit 20 rows. Turn work 90-degrees clockwise, and pick up and knit 10 sts along the left edge. Turn work 90-degrees clockwise, and pick up and knit 2 sts from CO edge—14 sts total.

**Set-Up Row (WS):** Knit all sts.

**Row 1 (RS):** K2, (YO, K1) to the last 2 sts, YO, K2—25 sts.

**Row 2:** K2, purl to the last 2 sts, K2.

**Row 3:** Knit all sts.

**Row 4:** Rep Row 2.

## BODY OF SHAWL

**Inc Row (RS):** K2, (k1, yo) to the last 3 sts, K3—45 sts.

**Row 1 (WS):** K2, purl to the last 2 sts, K2.

**Row 2:** Knit all sts.

Work Rows 1 and 2 another 3 times.

Work Row 1 once more.

Work Inc Row—85 sts.

**Next Row (WS):** K2, purl to the last 2 sts, K2.

Using the chart or written instructions, work Chart A once (14 rows).

Work Inc Row—165 sts.

**Next Row (WS):** K2, purl to the last 2 sts, k2.

Work Chart A twice (28 rows).

Work Inc Row—325 sts.

**Next Row (WS):** K2, purl to the last 2 sts, k2.

Using the chart or written instructions, work Chart B twice (28 rows).

Using the chart or written instructions, work Chart C twice (28 rows).

Work in garter st (knit every row) for 6 rows, ending with a WS row.

# Make It Your Own!

The charts for this pattern are all interchangeable. If you love one chart, you can use it in place of another one in the pattern. You can also add additional repeats of Chart C before working the last six rows of garter stitch.

If you want a giant snuggly shawl, you can easily modify this pattern to get one. Work as written until Chart C has been completed twice. Work another Increase Row to give a new stitch count of 645 sts. Work eight chart repeats of whatever chart you like. Finish off with the six rows of garter stitch and bind off.

**Remember:** Changing the number of repeats you work or changing the yarn weight will affect the finished size of your shawl as well as the amount of yarn needed to complete it.

## Written Instructions for Chart A

*Depending on what you prefer, follow either the chart or the written instructions below.*

**Rows 1–7 (RS):** Knit all sts.

**Rows 8, 10, and 12 (WS):** K2, purl to the last 2 sts, k2.

**Row 9 (RS):** K2, *k1, yo, ssk, k3, k2tog, yo; rep from * to last 3 sts, k3.

**Row 11:** K2, *k2, yo, ssk, k1, k2tog, yo, k1; rep from * to last 3 sts, k3.

**Row 13:** K2, *k3, yo, CDD, yo, k2; rep from * to last 3 sts, k3.

**Row 14:** K2, purl to the last 2 sts, k2.

## Written Instructions for Chart B

*Depending on what you prefer, follow either the chart or the written instructions below.*

**Rows 1–7 (RS):** Knit all sts.

**Rows 8, 10, and 12 (WS):** K2, purl to the last 2 sts, k2.

**Row 9 (RS):** K2, *k1, yo, k2, CDD, k2, yo; rep from * to last 3 sts, k3.

**Row 11:** K2, *k2, yo, k1, CDD, k1, yo, k1; rep from * to last 3 sts, k3.

**Row 13:** K2, *k3, yo, CDD, yo, k2; rep from * to last 3 sts, k3.

**Row 14:** K2, purl to the last 2 sts, k2.

## Written Instructions for Chart C

*Depending on what you prefer, follow either the chart or the written instructions below.*

**Rows 1–7 (RS):** Knit all sts.

**Rows 8, 10, and 12 (WS):** K2, purl to the last 2 sts, k2.

**Row 9 (RS):** K2, *k1, yo, k2, CDD, k2, yo; rep from * to last 3 sts, k3.

**Row 11:** K2, *yo, ssk, yo, k1, CDD, k1, yo, k1; rep from * to last 3 sts, k3.

**Row 13:** K2, *k1, yo, ssk, yo, CDD, yo, k2tog, yo; rep from * to last 3 sts, k3.

**Row 14:** K2, purl to the last 2 sts, k2.

## FINISHING

BO loosely kwise on RS. Block shawl to finished measurements given at beg of patt. With tapestry needle, weave in ends.

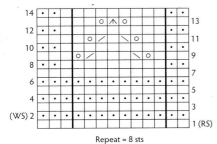

**CHEYENNE CHART A**

Repeat = 8 sts

### LEGEND

|  | K on RS, P on WS |  | K2tog |
| --- | --- | --- | --- |
| • | P on RS, K on WS |  | Ssk |
| o | YO |  | CDD |

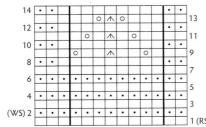

**CHEYENNE CHART B**

Repeat = 8 sts

### LEGEND

|  | K on RS, P on WS |  | K2tog |
| --- | --- | --- | --- |
| • | P on RS, K on WS |  | Ssk |
| o | YO |  |  |
|  | CDD |  |  |

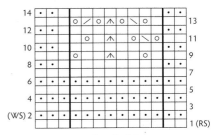

**CHEYENNE CHART C**

Repeat = 8 sts

### LEGEND

|  | K on RS, P on WS |  | K2tog |
| --- | --- | --- | --- |
| • | P on RS, K on WS |  | Ssk |
| o | YO |  | CDD |

# Ardor

Garter-stitch shawls are a great introduction to shawl knitting. Watch the easy garter-stitch portion grow on your needles, and then add a simple lace detail at the end. Try knitting one with a semisolid sock yarn for a rich, cozy shawl.

## FINISHED MEASUREMENTS

- 54" wide × 25" deep (137.2 × 63.5cm)

## MATERIALS

- 425 yards (388.6mm) of fingering weight yarn
- US Size 5 (3.75mm) circular needle, 32" (81.3cm) cable or longer, or size required for gauge
- Tapestry needle
- Blocking supplies

## YARN INFORMATION

- Sample uses 1 skein of Solemate from Lorna's Laces (55% superwash merino/30% Outlast viscose/15% nylon; 3.5oz/100g; 425 yds/388.6m) in color Kerfuffle

## GAUGE

- 20 sts and 34 rows = 4" (10.2cm) in St st, blocked
- *Gauge is not critical for this pattern; however, a different gauge will affect the finished size of the project as well as the amount of yarn needed.*

## PATTERN NOTES

- This project is worked mostly in garter stitch. As such, you may find it helpful to use a locking stitch marker to mark the right side of your project.

**The lace on this shawl looks a little like waves to me. Perhaps this is the perfect shawl for cool nights near the water.**

## BODY OF SHAWL

Work garter-tab CO as follows:

CO 3 sts. Knit 6 rows. Turn work 90-degrees clockwise and pick up and knit 3 sts along the left edge. Turn work 90-degrees clockwise and pick up and knit 3 sts from CO edge—9 sts total.

**Row 1 (RS):** K3, yo, k1, yo, k1 (center st, mark with st marker(s) if you like), yo, k1, yo, k3—13 sts.

**Row 2 (WS):** Knit all sts.

**Row 3:** K3, yo, knit to center st, yo, k1, yo, knit to last 3 sts, yo, k3—17 sts.

Work Rows 2 and 3 another 38 times—169 sts.

Rep Row 2 once more.

## LACE EDGING

Using the chart or written instructions, work Chart A between st markers on each half of shawl twice—205 sts after first rep; 241 sts after second rep.

Using the chart or written instructions, work Chart B between st markers on each half of shawl—269 sts.

### Written Instructions for Chart A

*Depending on what you prefer, follow either the chart or the written instructions below.*

**Rows 1 and 3 (RS):** K3, yo, knit to center st, yo, k1, yo, knit to last 3 sts, yo, k3.

**Rows 2 and 4 (WS):** Knit all sts.

**Row 5:** K3, yo, k2, *ssk, k4, yo, k1, yo, k2tog; rep from * to 2 sts before center st, k2, yo, k1 (center st, yo, k2, **ssk, yo, k1, yo, k4, k2tog; rep from ** to last 5 sts, k2, yo, k3.

**Rows 6, 8, 10, and 12:** K3, purl to last 3 sts, k3.

**Row 7:** K3, yo, k3, *ssk, k3, (yo, k1) twice, k2tog; rep from * to 3 sts from center st, k3, yo, k1, yo, k3, **ssk, (k1, yo) twice, k3, k2tog; rep from ** to last 6 sts, k3, yo, k3.

**Row 9:** K3, yo, k4, *ssk, k2, yo, k1, yo, k2, k2tog; rep from * to 4 sts before center st, k4, yo, k1, yo, k4, **ssk, k2, yo, k1, yo, k2, k2tog; rep from ** to last 7 sts, k4, yo, k3.

**Row 11:** K3, yo, k2, yo, ssk, yo, k1, *ssk, (k1, yo) twice, k3, k2tog; rep from * to 5 sts before center st, k1, yo, k2tog, yo, k2, yo, k1, yo, k2, ssk, yo, k1, **ssk, k3, (yo, k1) twice, k2tog; rep from ** to last 8 sts, k1, yo, k2tog, yo, k2, yo, k3.

# Make It Bigger!

With extra yarn, you can repeat the 14 rows of Chart A as many times as you like before moving to Chart B.

**Row 13:** (k3, yo) twice, ssk, yo, k2, *ssk, yo, k1, yo, k4, k2tog; rep from * to 7 sts before center st, k2, yo, k2tog, yo, k3, yo, k1, yo, k3, yo, ssk, yo, k2, **ssk, k4, yo, k1, yo, k2tog; rep from ** to last 10 sts, k2, yo, k2tog, (yo, k3) twice.

**Row 14:** K3, purl to last 3 sts, k3.

Rep Rows 1–14 for patt.

## Written Instructions for Chart B

*Depending on what you prefer, follow either the chart or the written instructions below.*

**Rows 1 and 3 (RS):** K3, yo, knit to center st, yo, k1, yo, knit to last 3 sts, yo, k3.

**Rows 2 and 4 (WS):** Knit all sts.

**Row 5:** K3, yo, k2, *ssk, yo, k1, yo, sk2p, yo, k1, yo, k2tog; rep from * to 2 sts before the center st, k2, yo, k1, yo, k2, **ssk, yo, k1, yo, sk2p, yo, k1, yo, k2tog; rep from ** to last 5 sts, k2, yo, k3.

**Rows 6, 8, 10, and 12:** K3, purl to last 3 sts, k3.

**Row 7:** K3, yo, k1, yo, k2tog, *ssk, yo, k1, yo, sk2p, yo, k1, yo, k2tog; rep from * to 3 sts before center st, ssk, (yo, k1) 3 times, yo, k2tog, **ssk, yo, k1, yo, sk2p, yo, k1, yo, k2tog; rep from ** to last 6 sts, ssk, yo, k1, yo, k3.

**Row 9:** K3, yo, k2, yo, k2tog, *ssk, yo, k1, yo, sk2p, yo, k1, yo, k2tog; rep from * to 4 sts before center st, ssk, yo, k2, yo, k1, yo, k2, yo, k2tog, **ssk, yo, k1, yo, sk2p, yo, k1, yo, k2tog; rep from ** to last 7 sts, ssk, yo, k2, yo, k3.

**Row 11:** (k3, yo) twice, k2tog, *ssk, yo, k1, yo, sk2p, yo, k1, yo, k2tog; rep from * to 5 sts before center st, ssk, yo, k3, yo, k1, yo, k3, yo, k2tog, **ssk, yo, k1, yo, sk2p, yo, k1, yo, k2tog; rep from ** to last 8 sts, ssk, (yo, k3) twice.

## FINISHING

BO loosely kwise on WS. Block shawl to finished measurements given at beg of patt. With tapestry needle, weave in ends.

### ARDOR CHART A

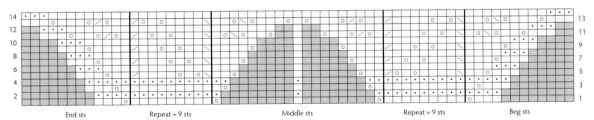

### ARDOR CHART B

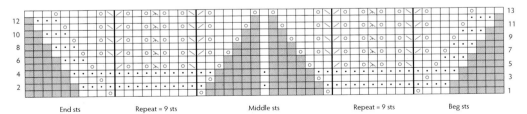

### LEGEND

|  |  |
|---|---|
| ☐ K on RS, P on WS | ⋊ SK2P |
| • P on RS, K on WS | ╱ K2tog |
| ○ YO | ▨ No stitch |
| ╲ Ssk | |

# Cinder

Here's a traditional top-down triangle shawl, with a twist—once the lace begins, it's time to ditch the center stitch and work a lovely lace pattern that looks like stacked bricks.

## FINISHED MEASUREMENTS

- 50" wide × 17" deep (127 × 43.2cm)

## MATERIALS

- 420 yds (384m) fingering-weight yarn
- US Size 4 (3.5mm) circular needle, 32" (81.3cm) cable or longer, or size required for gauge
- 4 stitch markers
- Tapestry needle
- Blocking supplies

## YARN INFORMATION

- Sample uses 1 skein of Adorn Sock from Three Irish Girls (80% merino/20% nylon; 3.5oz/100g; 430 yds/393.2m) in color Salt Spray

## GAUGE

- 22 sts and 32 rows = 4" (10.2cm) in St st, blocked
- *Gauge is not critical for this pattern; however, a different gauge will affect the finished size of the project as well as the amount of yarn needed.*

**The extra yarnovers at the edge of the shawl add interest to the simple lace pattern.**

## INSTRUCTIONS

Work garter-tab CO as follows:

CO 3 sts. Knit 6 rows. Turn work 90-degrees clockwise, and pick up and knit 3 sts along the left edge. Turn work 90-degrees clockwise, and pick up and knit 3 sts from CO edge—9 sts total.

## BODY OF SHAWL

**Row 1 (RS):** K3, pm, yo, k1, yo, pm, k1 (this is the center st), pm, yo, k1, yo, pm, k3—13 sts.

**Row 2 (WS):** K3, purl to last 3 sts slipping markers along the way, k3.

**Row 3:** K3, sm, yo, knit to next marker, yo, sm, k1, sm, yo, knit to last marker, yo, sm, k3—17 sts.

Work Rows 2 and 3 another 37 times.

Rep Row 2 once more—165 sts.

**Next Row (RS):** K3, sm, yo, k2, m1, knit to next marker, yo, sm, k1, sm, yo, knit to 2 sts before last marker, m1, k2, yo, sm, k3—171 sts.

**Next Row (WS):** K3, purl to last 3 sts removing markers along the way, k3.

## LACE EDGING

Using the charts or written instructions for the charts, work charts as follows:

Chart A—189 sts.

Chart B—207 sts.

Chart A—225 sts.

Chart B—243 sts.

Chart A—261 sts.

Work Rows 1–7 only of Chart B—277 sts.

**Next Row (WS):** K2, kfb, knit to end—278 sts.

**Next Row (RS):** K1, *yo twice, sk2p; rep from * to last st, yo twice, K1.

**Next Row:** K1, *(k1, p1) twice into double yo, k1; rep from * to last 3 sts, (k1, p1) twice into double yo, k1.

# Make It Bigger!

With additional yarn, continue to repeat Charts A and B to desired size, ending with Row 7 of Chart B. Work the last 3 rows of lace edge as written.

## Written Instructions for Chart A

*Depending on what you prefer, follow either the chart or the written instructions below.*

**Row 1 (RS):** K3, yo, knit to last 3 sts, yo, k3.

**Row 2 and all even-numbered rows (WS):** K4, yo, purl to last 4 sts, yo, k4.

**Row 3:** K3, yo, k2, *k3, yo, sk2p, yo; rep from * to last 8 sts, k5, yo, k3.

**Row 5:** K3, yo, knit to last 3 sts, yo, k3.

**Row 7:** K3, yo, k1, yo, k2tog, yo, k3, *yo, sk2p, yo, k3; rep from * to last 12 sts, yo, sk2p, yo, k3, yo, ssk, yo, k1, yo, k3.

**Row 8:** K4, yo, purl to last 4 sts, yo, k4.

## Written Instructions for Chart B

*Depending on what you prefer, follow either the chart or the written instructions below.*

**Row 1 (RS):** K3, yo, knit to last 3 sts, yo, k3.

**Row 2 and all even-numbered rows (WS):** K4, yo, purl to last 4 sts, yo, k4.

**Row 3:** K3, yo, k2, *yo, sk2p, yo, k3; rep from * to last 8 sts, yo, sk2p, yo, k2, yo, k3.

**Row 5:** K3, yo, knit to last 3 sts, yo, k3.

**Row 7:** K3, yo, k4, yo, k2tog, yo, *k3, yo, sk2p, yo; rep from * to last 12 sts, k3, yo, ssk, yo, k4, yo, k3.

**Row 8:** K4, yo, purl to last 4 sts, yo, k4.

## FINISHING

BO loosely kwise on RS. Block shawl to finished measurements given at beg of patt. With tapestry needle, weave in ends.

CINDER CHART A

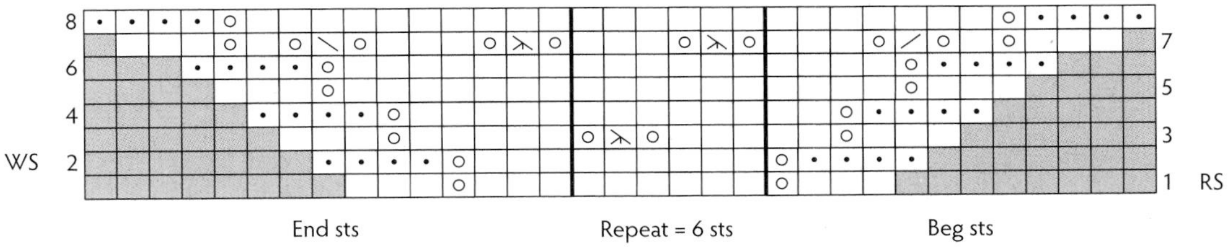

End sts    Repeat = 6 sts    Beg sts

CINDER CHART B

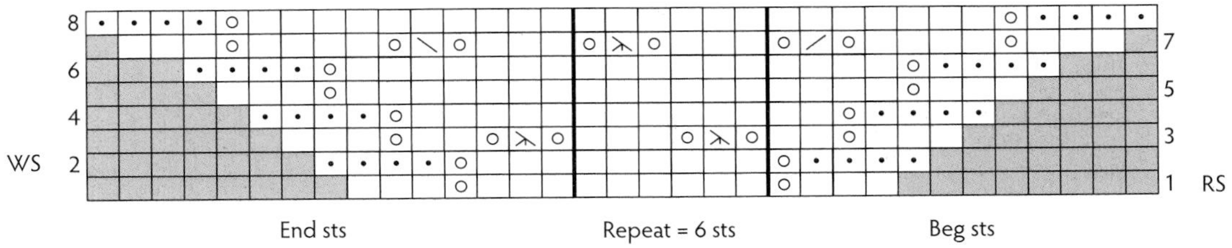

End sts    Repeat = 6 sts    Beg sts

LEGEND

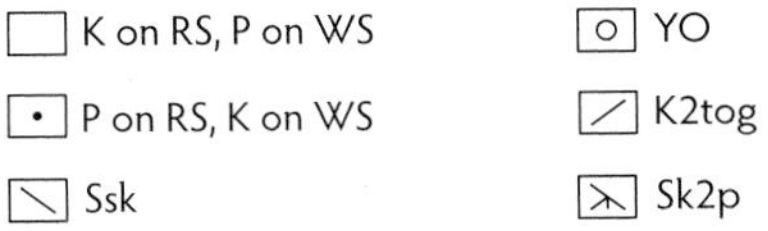

- ☐ K on RS, P on WS
- • P on RS, K on WS
- ◻ Ssk
- ○ YO
- ╱ K2tog
- ⤢ Sk2p

# Laplace

This top-down crescent shawl features garter stitch worked between lace stitches. Worsted-weight yarn makes this a very quick project!

## FINISHED MEASUREMENTS
- 74" wide × 19" deep (188 × 48.3cm)

## MATERIALS
- 600 yds (548.6m) worsted-weight yarn
- US Size 8 (5.0mm) circular needle, 32" (81.3cm) cable or longer, or size required for gauge
- Tapestry needle
- Blocking supplies

## YARN INFORMATION
- Sample uses 3 skeins of Cadence from Hazel Knits (100% superwash merino wool; 3.9oz/110g; 200 yds/182.9m) in the color Low Tide

## GAUGE
- 16 sts and 28 rows = 4" (10.2cm) in garter st, blocked
- *Gauge is not critical for this pattern; however, a different gauge will affect the finished size of the project as well as the amount of yarn needed.*

**Garter stitch and lace together again—my favorite!**

## INSTRUCTIONS

Work garter-tab CO as follows:
CO 3 sts. Knit 10 rows. Turn work
90-degrees clockwise, and pick up
and knit 5 sts along the left edge.
Turn work 90-degrees clockwise,
and pick up and knit 3 sts from CO
edge—11 sts total.

**Row 1 (WS):** K3, p5, k3.

**Row 2 (RS):** K3, (yo, k1) to last 3
sts, yo, k3—17 sts.

**Row 3:** K2, yo, k1, purl to the last 3
sts, k1, yo, k2—19 sts.

**Row 4:** K3, yo, knit to the last 3 sts,
yo, k3—21 sts.

**Row 5:** Rep Row 3—23 sts.

| STITCH COUNT FOR BODY OF SHAWL | |
|---|---|
| Rep 1 of Chart A | 39 sts |
| Rep 2 of Chart A | 55 sts |
| Rep 3 of Chart A | 71 sts |
| Rep 4 of Chart A | 87 sts |
| Rep 5 of Chart A | 103 sts |
| Rep 6 of Chart A | 119 sts |
| Rep 7 of Chart A | 135 sts |
| Rep 8 of Chart A | 151 sts |
| Rep 9 of Chart A | 167 sts |
| Rep 10 of Chart A | 183 sts |
| Chart B | 199 sts |

## BODY OF SHAWL

Using the chart or written instructions, work Chart A 10 times total—183 sts.

Using the chart or written instructions, work Chart B once—199 sts.

### Written Instructions for Chart A

*Depending on what you prefer, follow either the chart or the written instructions below.*

**Row 1 (RS):** K3, yo, *k3, ssk, k3, yo, k1, yo, k3, k2tog, k2; rep from * to last 4 sts, k1, yo, k3.

**Row 2 (WS):** K2, yo, k3, *k2, p11, k3; rep from * to last 4 sts, k2, yo, k2.

**Row 3:** K3, yo, k2, *k3, ssk, k2, yo, k3, yo, k2tog, k2; rep from * to last 6 sts, k3, yo, k3.

**Row 4:** K2, yo, k1, p1, k3, *k2, p11, k3; rep from * to last 6 sts, k2, p1, k1, yo, k2.

**Row 5:** K3, yo, k4, *k3, ssk, k1, yo, k5, yo, k1, k2tog, k2; rep from * to last 8 sts, k5, yo, k3.

**Row 6:** K2, yo, k1, p3, k3, *k2, p11, k3; rep from * to last 8 sts, k2, p3, k1, yo, k2.

**Row 7:** K3, yo, k6, *k3, ssk, yo, k7, yo, k2tog, k2; rep from * to last 10 sts, k7, yo, k3.

# Make It Your Own!

This shawl is easy to adjust to the size you want, making it a great project for substituting yarn weights. Work Chart A to the desired length, and then work Chart B once.

You can also work the Garter Stitch Border to desired length by repeating Rows 1 and 2 to the desired length. Remember: Changing the number of repeats you work or changing the yarn weight will affect the finished size of your shawl as well as the amount of yarn needed to complete it.

**Row 8:** K2, yo, k1, p5, k3, *k2, p11, k3; rep from * to last 10 sts, k2, p5, k1, yo, k2.
Rep Rows 1–8 for patt.

## Written Instructions for Chart B

*Depending on what you prefer, follow either the chart or the written instructions below.*

**Row 1 (RS):** K3, yo, *k3, ssk, k3, yo, k1, yo, k3, k2tog, k2; rep from * to last 4 sts, k1, yo, k3.

**Row 2 (WS):** K2, yo, k3, *k2, p5, k1, p5, k3; rep from * to last 4 sts, k2, yo, k2.

**Row 3:** K3, yo, k2, *k3, ssk, k2, yo, k3, yo, k2tog, k2; rep from * to last 6 sts, k3, yo, k3.

**Row 4:** K2, yo, k1, p1, k3, *k2, p4, k3, p4, k3; rep from * to last 6 sts, k2, p1, k1, yo, k2.

**Row 5:** K3, yo, k4, *k3, ssk, k1, yo, k5, yo, k1, k2tog, k2; rep from * to last 8 sts, k5, yo, k3.

**Row 6:** K2, yo, k1, p3, k3, *k2, p3, k5, p3, k3; rep from * to last 8 sts, k2, p3, k1, yo, k2.

**Row 7:** K3, yo, k6, *k3, ssk, yo, k7, yo, k2tog, k2; rep from * to last 10 sts, k7, yo, k3.

**Row 8:** K2, yo, k1, p5, k3, *k2, p2, k7, p2, k3; rep from * to last 10 sts, k2, p5, k1, yo, k2.

## GARTER-STITCH BORDER

**Row 1 (RS):** K3, yo, knit to the last 3 sts, yo, k3—201 sts.

**Row 2 (WS):** K2, yo, knit to the last 2 sts, yo, K2—203 sts.
Rep last two rows another 11 times—247 sts.

## FINISHING

BO loosely kwise on RS. Block shawl to finished measurements given at beg of patt. With tapestry needle, weave in ends.

LAPLACE CHART A

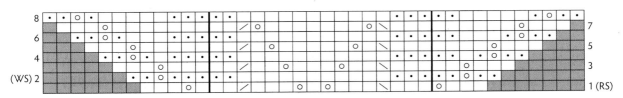

Repeat = 16 sts

LAPLACE CHART B

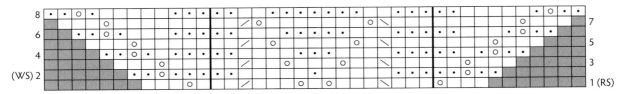

Repeat = 16 sts

LEGEND

☐ K on RS, P on WS    ◿ K2tog

• P on RS, K on WS    ◺ Ssk

○ YO    ▨ No stitch

# Violetear Cowl

Show off the Old Shale–style pattern in a garment that's a clever twist on the traditional cowl. The piece is worked flat, and a partial seam is added at the end to give you a variety of ways to wear it.

## FINISHED MEASUREMENTS

- 60" × 16" (152.4 × 40.6cm), before seaming

## MATERIALS

- 850 yds (777.2m) fingering-weight yarn
- US Size 5 (3.75mm) circular needle, 32" (81.3cm) cable or longer, or size required for gauge
- Tapestry needle
- Blocking supplies

## YARN INFORMATION

- Sample uses 3 skeins of Silk Crush from SweetGeorgia Yarns (50% superwash merino/50% silk; 4oz/114g; 375 yds/342.9m) in color Mist

## GAUGE

- 20 sts and 28 rows = 4" (10.2cm) in St st, blocked
- *Gauge is not critical for this pattern; however, a different gauge will affect the finished size of the project as well as the amount of yarn needed.*

**By working the piece flat and then seaming the ends together, you create an accessory that can be worn in a variety of interesting ways.**

## INSTRUCTIONS

CO 91 sts.

**Next Row (WS):** Knit all sts.

Using the chart or written instructions for chart, work Chart until piece measures approximately 54" (137.2cm) from CO edge, ending with Row 5.

**Final Row (WS):** Knit all sts.

### Written Instructions for Chart

*Depending on what you prefer, follow either the chart or the written instructions below.*

**Row 1 (RS):** K3, *ssk 3 times, (yo, k1) 5 times, yo, k2tog 3 times; rep from * to last 3 sts, k3.

**Row 2 and all even-numbered rows (WS):** K3, purl to last 3 sts, K3.

**Row 3:** Knit all sts.

**Row 5:** Rep Row 1.

**Row 7:** K3, *p3, k3, p5, k3, p3; rep from * to last 3 sts, k3.

**Row 9:** Rep Row 7.

**Row 11:** Rep Row 7.

**Row 12:** K3, purl to last 3 sts, k3.

## FINISHING

BO loosely kwise on RS. Block shawl to finished measurements given at beg of patt. With tapestry needle, weave in ends.

With tapestry needle, weave in ends. Fold in half lengthwise (lining up CO and BO edges). Starting at CO/BO edge, whipstitch 6" (15.2cm) along one lengthwise edge. Leave remainder of edge unsewn.

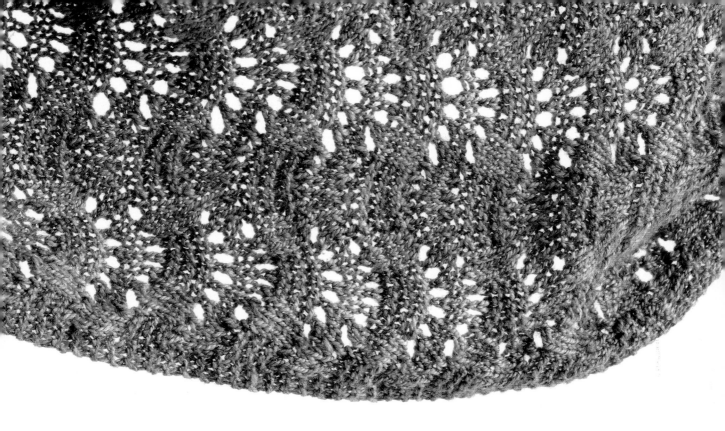

## VIOLETEAR COWL CHART

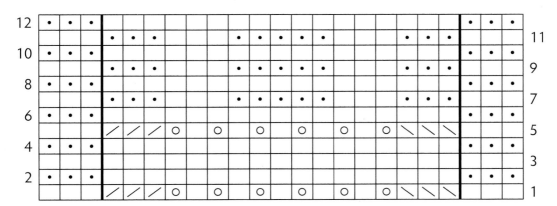

Repeat = 17 sts

# Violetear Shawl

I know that many knitters love bottom-up short-row shawls just as much as I do. I've designed many of them over the years, but this one is my favorite. The way the feather-and-fan lace flows into the garter-stitch body of the shawl makes me happy. I hope it makes you happy too!

## FINISHED MEASUREMENTS

- 62" wide × 12" deep (157.5 × 30.5cm)

## MATERIALS

- 600 yds (548.6m) fingering-weight yarn
- US Size 5 (3.75mm) circular needle, 32" (61cm) cable or longer, or size required for gauge
- Tapestry needle
- Blocking supplies

## YARN INFORMATION

- Sample uses 2 skeins of CashLuxe Fine from SweetGeorgia Yarns (70% superwash merino/20% cashmere/10% nylon; 4oz/114g; 400 yds/365.8m) in color Laurel

## GAUGE

- 16 sts and 32 rows = 4" (10.2cm) in garter st, blocked
- *Gauge is not critical for this pattern; however, a different gauge will affect the finished size of the project as well as the amount of yarn needed.*

**Small garter-stitch details within the Old Shale–style lace make this the ideal pattern to use in a shawl with a garter-stitch body.**

## INSTRUCTIONS

CO 363 sts.

**Set-Up Row (WS):** Knit all sts.

Using the chart or the written instructions for the char, work Chart A 3 times.

Using the chart or the written instructions for the char, work Chart B once—279 sts.

### Written Instructions for Chart A

*Depending on what you prefer, follow either the chart or the written instructions below.*

**Row 1 (RS):** K3, *ssk 3 times, (yo, k1) 5 times, yo, k2tog 3 times; rep from * to last 3 sts, k3.

**Row 2 and all even-numbered rows (WS):** K3, purl to last 3 sts, k3.

**Row 3:** Knit all sts.

**Row 5:** Rep Row 1.

**Rows 7, 9 and 11:** K3, *p3, k3, p5, k3, p3; rep from * to last 3 sts, k3.

**Row 12:** K3, purl to last 3 sts, k3.

### Written Instructions for Chart B

*Depending on what you prefer, follow either the chart or the written instructions below.*

**Row 1 (RS):** K3, *ssk 3 times, (yo, k1) 5 times, yo, k2tog 3 times; rep from * to last 3 sts, k3.

**Rows 2, 4, 6, 8, 10, 12, 14, and 16 (WS):** K3, purl to last 3 sts, k3.

**Row 3:** Knit all sts.

**Row 5:** Rep Row 1.

**Rows 7, 9, and 11:** K3, *p3, k3, p5, k3, p3; rep from * to last 3 sts, k3.

**Row 13:** K3, *ssk 3 times, (k1, yo) 4 times, k1, k2tog 3 times; rep from * to last 3 sts, k3.

**Row 15:** Knit all sts.

**Row 17:** K3, *ssk 3 times, (yo, K1) 3 times, yo, k2tog 3 times; rep from * to last 3 sts, k3.

**Row 18:** Knit all sts.

## SHORT-ROW SECTION

**Row 1 (RS):** K144, turn work—135 sts unworked.

**Row 2 (WS):** K9, turn work—135 sts unworked.

**Row 3:** K8, ssk, k4, turn work—130 sts unworked; 278 sts total.

**Row 4:** K8, k2tog, k4, turn work—130 sts unworked; 277 sts total.

**Row 5:** Knit to 1 st before gap (1 st before previous turning point), ssk, k4, turn work.

**Row 6:** Knit to 1 st before gap (1 st before previous turning point), k2tog, k4, turn work.

Repeat last two rows another 25 times. All sts have been worked—225 sts.

## FINISHING

BO loosely kwise on RS. Block shawl to finished measurements given at beg of patt. With tapestry needle, weave in ends.

## VIOLETEAR SHAWL CHART A

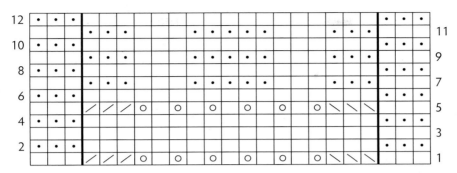

Repeat = 17 sts

## VIOLETEAR SHAWL CHART B

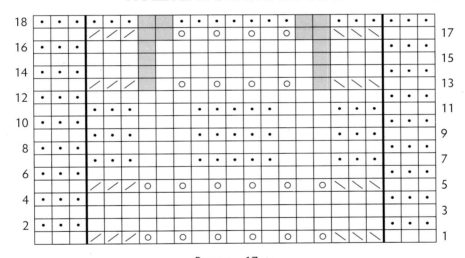

Repeat = 17 sts

## LEGEND

| | | |
|---|---|---|
| ☐ K on RS, P on WS | ◢ K2tog | |
| ⊡ P on RS, K on WS | ◣ SSK | |
| ⊙ YO | ▨ No stitch | |

# Garter Love

There's something about the garter stitch that just seems so cozy to me. It's probably one of the reasons I love it so much. This shawl is all about garter-stitch love! The simple body of the shawl transitions into the lace edge, where the garter stitch is the star.

**The simplicity and geometric elements of this shawl make it a delight to knit!**

## FINISHED MEASUREMENTS

- 52" wide × 20" deep (132.1 × 50.8cm)

## MATERIALS

- 395 yds (361.2m) fingering-weight yarn
- US Size 4 (3.5mm) circular needle, 32" (81.3cm) cable or longer, or size required for gauge
- 4 stitch markers
- Tapestry needle
- Blocking supplies

## YARN INFORMATION

- Sample uses 1 skein of Tosh Sock from Madelinetosh Hand-Dyed Yarns (100% superwash merino; 4oz/114g; 395 yds/361.2m) in color Cherry

## GAUGE

- 18 sts and 32 rows = 4" (10.2cm) in garter st, blocked
- *Gauge is not critical for this pattern; however, a different gauge will affect the finished size of the project as well as the amount of yarn needed.*

## PATTERN NOTES

- If using additional stitch markers to mark each stitch repeat, on some rows, the stitch markers will need to be rearranged. For this pattern, you'll need to rearrange these stitch markers on Row 19 of Chart A. For more information on this technique, see page 14.
- This project is worked mostly in garter stitch. As such, you may find it helpful to use a locking stitch marker to mark the right side of your project.

## BODY OF SHAWL

Work garter-tab CO as follows:

CO 3 sts. Knit 6 rows. Turn work 90-degrees clockwise, and pick up and knit 3 sts along the left edge. Turn work 90-degrees clockwise, and pick up and knit 3 sts from CO edge—9 sts total.

**Row 1 (RS):** K3, pm, yo, k1, yo, pm, k1 (center st), pm, yo, k1, yo, pm, k3—13 sts.

**Row 2 (WS):** K3, purl to last 3 sts, k3.

**Row 3:** K3, sm, yo, knit to next marker, yo, sm, k1, sm, yo, knit to last 3 sts, yo, sm, k3—17 sts.

Work Rows 2 and 3 another 46 times—201 sts.

Rep Row 2 once more.

## LACE EDGING

Continue working first 3 sts and last 3 sts in garter st (knit every row). Work the center st in St st (knit on RS, purl on WS).

Using the chart or written instructions, work Chart A between st markers on each half of shawl—249 sts.

Using the chart or written instructions, work Chart B between st markers on each half of shawl—269 sts.

### Written Instructions for Chart A

*Depending on what you prefer, follow either the chart or the written instructions below.*

**Row 1 (RS):** Yo, k1, *yo, ssk, k7, k2tog, yo, k1; rep from * to marker, yo.

**Row 2 (WS):** P1, *p3, k7, p2; rep from * to 2 sts before marker, p2.

**Row 3:** Yo, k2, *k1, yo, ssk, k5, k2tog, yo, k2; rep from * to last st before marker, k1, yo.

**Row 4:** P2, *p4, k5, p3; rep from * to 3 sts before marker, p3.

**Row 5:** Yo, k3, *k2, yo, ssk, k3, k2tog, yo, k3; rep from * to 2 sts before marker, k2, yo.

**Row 6:** P3, *p5, k3, p4; rep from * to 4 sts before marker, p4.

**Row 7:** Yo, k4, *k3, yo, ssk, k1, k2tog, yo, k4; rep from * to 3 sts before marker, k3, yo.

**Row 8:** P4, *p6, k1, p5; rep from * to 5 sts before marker, p5.

**Row 9:** Yo, k5, *k4, yo, sk2p, yo, k5; rep from * to 4 sts before marker, k4, yo.

**Row 10:** Purl all sts.

**Row 11:** Yo, k6, *k3, k2tog, yo, k1, yo, ssk, k4; rep from * to 5 sts before marker, k5, yo.

**Row 12:** P3, k3, *k4, p5, k3; rep from * to 7 sts before marker, k4, p3.

# Make It Bigger!

With extra yarn, you can add as many repeats of Chart A as you like before working Chart B.

**Row 13:** Yo, k2, yo, ssk, k3, *k2, k2tog, yo, k3, yo, ssk, k3; rep from * to 6 sts before marker, k2, k2tog, yo, k2, yo.

**Row 14:** P5, k2, *k3, p7, k2; rep from * to 8 sts before marker, k3, p5.

**Row 15:** Yo, k1, k2tog, yo, k1, yo, ssk, k2, *k1, k2tog, yo, k5, yo, ssk, k2; rep from * to 7 sts before marker, k1, k2tog, yo, k1, yo, ssk, k1, yo.

**Row 16:** P7, k1, *k2, p9, k1; rep from * to 9 sts before marker, k2, p7.

**Row 17:** Yo, k1, yo, k2tog, yo, k3, yo, ssk, k1, *k2tog, yo, k7, yo, ssk, k1; rep from * to 8 sts before marker, k2tog, yo, k3, yo, ssk, yo, k1, yo.

**Row 18:** P10, *k1, p11; rep from * to 11 sts before marker, k1, p10.

**Row 19:** Yo, k2, yo, k2tog, yo, k5, yo, sk2p, *yo, k9, yo, sk2p; rep from * to 9 sts before marker, yo, k5, yo, ssk, yo, k2, yo.

**Row 20:** Purl all sts.

Rep Rows 1–20 for patt.

## Written Instructions for Chart B

*Depending on what you prefer, follow either the chart or the written instructions below.*

**Row 1 (RS):** Yo, k1, *yo, ssk, k7, k2tog, yo, k1; rep from * to marker, yo.

**Row 2 (WS):** P1, *p3, k7, p2; rep from * to 2 sts before marker, p2.

**Row 3:** Yo, k2, *k1, yo, ssk, k5, k2tog, yo, k2; rep from * to last st before marker, k1, yo.

**Row 4:** P2, *p4, k5, p3; rep from * to 3 sts before marker, p3.

**Row 5:** Yo, k2tog, yo, k1, *(yo, ssk) twice, k3, (k2tog, yo) twice, k1; rep from * to 2 sts before marker, yo, ssk, yo.

**Row 6:** P3, *p5, k3, p4; rep from * to 4 sts before marker, p4.

**Row 7:** Yo, k2tog, yo, k2, *k1, (yo, ssk) twice, k1, (k2tog, yo) twice, k2; rep from * to 3 sts before marker, k1, yo, ssk, yo.

**Row 8:** P4, *p6, k1, p5; rep from * to 5 sts before marker, p5.

**Row 9:** Yo, (k2tog, yo) twice, k1, *(yo, ssk) twice, yo, sk2p, yo, (k2tog, yo) twice, k1; rep from * to 4 sts before marker, (yo, ssk) twice, yo.

## FINISHING

BO loosely kwise on WS. Block shawl to finished measurements given at beg of patt. With tapestry needle, weave in ends.

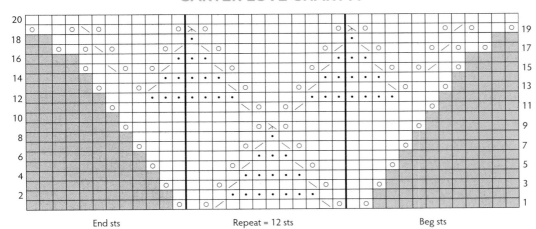

GARTER LOVE CHART A

End sts    Repeat = 12 sts    Beg sts

GARTER LOVE CHART B

End sts    Repeat = 12 sts    Beg sts

LEGEND

| | | | |
|---|---|---|---|
| ⊡ YO | | ⊡ P on RS, K on WS | |
| ☐ K on RS, P on WS | | ⋊ SK2P | |
| ⧵ Ssk | | ▨ No stitch | |
| ⧸ K2tog | | | |

# Monarda

Featuring garter stitch and lace, this shawl offers lots to love. Started from the top center and worked outward, this lovely lace pattern will leave you wanting to make more than one.

## FINISHED MEASUREMENTS
- 56" wide × 18" deep (142.2 × 45.7cm)

## MATERIALS
- 395 yds (361.2m) fingering-weight yarn
- US Size 4 (3.5mm) circular needle, 32" (81.3cm) cable or longer, or size required for gauge
- Tapestry needle
- Blocking supplies

## YARN INFORMATION
- Sample uses 1 skein of Tosh Sock from Madelintosh (100% superwash merino wool; 3.5oz/100g; 395 yds/361.2m) in color Posy

## GAUGE
- 20 sts and 28 rows = 4" (10.2cm) in St st, blocked
- *Gauge is not critical for this pattern; however, a different gauge will affect the finished size of the project as well as the amount of yarn needed.*

## PATTERN NOTES
- If using stitch markers to mark each stitch repeat, on some rows, the stitch markers will need to be rearranged. For this pattern, you'll need to rearrange these stitch markers Row 9 of Chart B. For more information on this technique, see page 14.

**Mix garter and lace stitches together for a favorite combination!**

## INSTRUCTIONS

CO 5 sts.

**Row 1 (RS):** (K1, kfb) twice, k1—7 sts.

**Row 2 (WS):** K2, (YO, k1) 3 times, YO, k2—11 sts.

**Row 3:** K2, YO, k1, YO, ssk, k1, k2tog, YO, k1, YO, k2—13 sts.

**Row 4:** K2, YO, purl to last 2 sts, YO, k2—15 sts.

**Row 5:** K2, YO, k4, YO, sk2p, YO, k4, YO, k2—17 sts.

**Row 6:** K2, YO, k2, purl to last 4 sts, k2, YO, k2—19 sts.

## BODY OF SHAWL

Using the chart or written instructions for chart, work Chart A 7 times—215 sts.

Using the chart or written instructions for chart, work Chart B once—243 sts.

Using the chart or written instructions for chart, work Chart C once—253 sts.

| STITCH COUNTS FOR CHART A REPEATS | |
|---|---|
| First rep of Chart A | 47 sts |
| Second rep of Chart A | 75 sts |
| Third rep of Chart A | 103 sts |
| Fourth rep of Chart A | 131 sts |
| Fifth rep of Chart A | 159 sts |
| Sixth rep of Chart A | 187 sts |
| Seventh rep of Chart A | 215 sts |

# Make It Bigger!

With additional yarn, continue to repeat Chart A to desired size before moving on to Chart B.

## Written Instructions for Chart A

*Depending on what you prefer, follow either the chart or the written instructions below.*

**Row 1 (RS):** K2, yo, k1, *k2, ssk, k2, yo, k1, yo, k2, k2tog, k3; rep from * to last 2 sts, yo, k2.

**Row 2 (WS):** K2, yo, k1, *k3, p9, k2; rep from * to last 4 sts, k2, yo, k2.

**Row 3:** K2, yo, k3, *k2, ssk, k2, yo, k1, yo, k2, k2tog, k3; rep from * to last 4 sts, k2, yo, k2.

**Row 4:** K2, yo, p1, k2, *k3, p9, k2; rep from * to last 6 sts, k3, p1, yo, k2.

**Row 5:** K2, yo, k5, *k2, ssk, k2, yo, k1, yo, k2, k2tog, k3; rep from * to last 6 sts, k4, yo, k2.

**Row 6:** K2, yo, p3, k2, *k3, p9, k2; rep from * to last 8 sts, k3, p3, yo, k2.

**Row 7:** K2, yo, k2, k2tog, yo, k3, *k2, yo, ssk, k5, k2tog, yo, k3; rep from * to last 8 sts, k2, yo, ssk, k2, yo, k2.

**Row 8:** K2, yo, p5, k2, *k3, p9, k2; rep from * to last 10 sts, k3, p5, yo, k2.

**Row 9:** K2, yo, k3, k2tog, yo, k4, *k3, yo, ssk, k3, k2tog, yo, k4; rep from * to last 10 sts, k3, yo, ssk, k3, yo, k2.

**Row 10:** K2, yo, p7, k2, *k3, p9, k2; rep from * to last 12 sts, k3, p7, yo, k2.

**Row 11:** K2, yo, k1, yo, ssk, k1, k2tog, yo, k5, *k4, yo, ssk, k1, k2tog, yo, k5; rep from * to last 12 sts, k4, yo, ssk, k1, k2tog, yo, k1, yo, k2.

**Row 12:** K2, yo, p9, k2, *k3, p9, k2; rep from * to last 14 sts, k3, p9, yo, k2.

**Row 13:** K2, yo, k4, yo, sk2p, yo, k6, *k5, yo, sk2p, yo, k6; rep from * to last 14 sts, k5, yo, sk2p, yo, k4, yo, k2.

**Row 14:** K2, yo, k2, p9, k2, *k3, p9, k2; rep from * to last 16 sts, k3, p9, k2, yo, k2.

Rep Rows 1–14 for patt.

## Written Instructions for Chart B

*Depending on what you prefer, follow either the chart or the written instructions below.*

**Row 1 (RS):** K2, yo, k1, *k3, k2tog, yo, k3, yo, ssk, k4; rep from * to last 2 sts, yo, k2.

**Row 2 (WS):** K2, yo, k1, *k3, p9, k2; rep from * to last 4 sts, k2, yo, k2.

**Row 3:** K2, yo, k3, *k2, k2tog, yo, k5, yo, ssk, k3; rep from * to last 4 sts, k2, yo, k2.

**Row 4:** K2, yo, p1, k2, *k3, p9, k2; rep from * to last 6 sts, k3, p1, yo, k2.

**Row 5:** K2, yo, k1, yo, ssk, k2, *k1, k2tog, yo, k7, yo, ssk, k2; rep from * to last 6 sts, k1, k2tog, yo, k1, yo, k2.

**Row 6:** K2, yo, p4, k1, *k2, p11, k1; rep from * to last 8 sts, k2, p4, yo, k2.

**Row 7:** K2, yo, k4, yo, ssk, k1, *k2tog, yo, k9, yo, ssk, k1; rep from * to last 8 sts, k2tog, yo, k4, yo, k2.

**Row 8:** K2, yo, p7, *k1, p13; rep from * to last 10 sts, k1, p7, yo, k2.

**Row 9:** K2, yo, k7, yo, sk2p, *yo, k11, yo, sk2p; rep from * to last 9 sts, yo, k7, yo, k2.

**Row 10:** K2, yo, purl to last 2 sts, yo, k2.

**Row 11:** K2, yo, k3, k2tog, k5, yo, k1, *yo, k5, sk2p, k5, yo, k1; rep from * to last 12 sts, yo, k5, ssk, k3, yo, k2.

**Row 12:** K2, yo, purl to last 2 sts, yo, k2.

**Row 13:** K2, yo, k5, k2tog, k5, yo, k1, *yo, k5, sk2p, k5, yo, k1; rep from * to last 14 sts, yo, k5, ssk, k5, yo, k2.

**Row 14:** K2, yo, purl to last 2 sts, yo, k2.

## Written Instructions for Chart C

*Depending on what you prefer, follow either the chart or the written instructions below.*

**Row 1 (RS):** K2, yo, k1, *yo, k5, sk2p, k5, yo, k1; rep from * to last 2 sts, yo, k2.

**Row 2 (WS):** K2, yo, purl to last 2 sts, yo, k2.

**Row 3:** K2, yo, k3, *yo, k5, sk2p, k5, yo, k1; rep from * to last 4 sts, k2, yo, k2.

**Row 4:** K2, yo, purl to last 2 sts, yo, k2.

**Row 5:** K2, yo, k5, *yo, k5, sk2p, k5, yo, k1; rep from * to last 6 sts, k4, yo, k2.

## FINISHING

BO loosely kwise on WS. Block shawl to finished measurements given at beg of patt. With tapestry needle, weave in ends.

## MONARDA CHART A

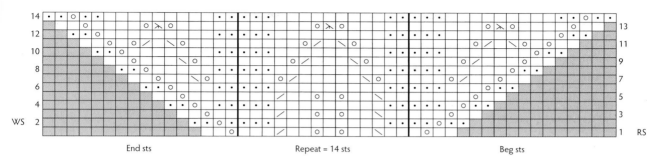

End sts          Repeat = 14 sts          Beg sts

## MONARDA CHART B

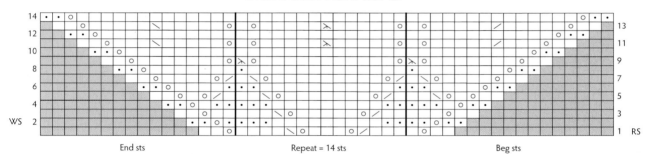

End sts          Repeat = 14 sts          Beg sts

## MONARDA CHART C

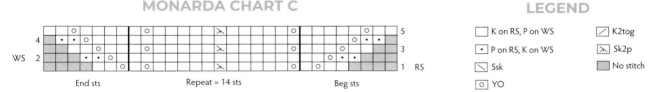

End sts          Repeat = 14 sts          Beg sts

### LEGEND

| | |
|---|---|
| ☐ K on RS, P on WS | ◢ K2tog |
| • P on RS, K on WS | ⅄ Sk2p |
| ◥ Ssk | ▨ No stitch |
| ○ YO | |

# Garnett

A thick Aran-weight yarn is paired with triangle shaping in garter stitch for this shawl. This is the perfect piece when you want to be warm and cozy.

## FINISHED MEASUREMENTS
- 70" wide × 18" deep (177.8 x 45.7cm)

## MATERIALS
- 360 yds (329.2m) Aran-weight yarn
- US Size 8 (5.0mm) circular needle, 32" (81.3cm) cable or longer, or size required for gauge
- 4 stitch markers
- Tapestry needle
- Blocking supplies

## YARN INFORMATION
- Sample uses 2 skeins of Cole from Anzula Luxury Fibers (70% silk/30% camel; 4oz/114g; 180 yds/164.6m) in color Seabreeze

## GAUGE
- 14 sts and 28 rows = 4" (10.2cm) in garter st, blocked
- *Gauge is not critical for this pattern; however, a different gauge will affect the finished size of the project as well as the amount of yarn needed.*

## PATTERN NOTES
- This project is worked primarily in garter stitch. You may find it helpful to use an additional locking stitch marker to indicate the right side of the work.

**Another shawl with garter stitch and lace? What can I say—it will forever be my favorite combination of stitches to knit.**

## INSTRUCTIONS

Work garter-tab CO as follows:

CO 3 sts. Knit 6 rows. Turn work 90-degrees clockwise, and pick up and knit 3 sts along the left edge. Turn work 90-degrees clockwise, and pick up and knit 3 sts from CO edge—9 sts total.

**Row 1 (WS):** K3, pm, k1, pm, k1 (this is the center st), pm, k1, pm, k3.

**Row 2 (RS):** K3, sm, yo, knit to marker, yo, sm, k1, sm, yo, knit to last marker, yo, k3—13 sts.

**Row 3:** Knit all sts.

Rep Rows 2 and 3 another 31 times (32 times total)—137 sts.

Rep Row 2 once more—141 sts.

**Next Row (WS):** K3, remove marker, knit to next marker, remove marker, kfb, remove marker, knit to final marker, remove marker, K3—142 sts.

Work charts as follows:

Chart A—158 sts

Chart B—174 sts

Chart A—190 sts

Chart B—206 sts

Chart A—222 sts

Chart B—238 sts

Work final garter-st band as follows:

(Worked same on both RS and WS)

**Rows 1–8 (RS):** K3, yo, knit to the last 3 sts, yo, k3—254 sts.

### Written Instructions for Chart A

*Depending on what you prefer, follow either the chart or the written instructions below.*

**Row 1 (RS):** K3, yo, *k8, (k2tog, yo) 4 times; rep from * to last 11 sts, k8, yo, k3.

**Row 2 (WS):** K3, yo, k9, *p8, k8; rep from * to last 4 sts, k1, yo, k3.

**Row 3:** K3, yo, k2, *k8, (k2tog, yo) 4 times; rep from * to last 13 sts, k10, yo, k3.

**Row 4:** K3, yo, k1, p2, k8, *p8, k8; rep from * to last 6 sts, p2, k1, yo, k3.

# Make It Your Own!

You can easily adjust the size of this shawl. Repeat Charts A and B (i.e., A, B, A, B, etc.) to the desired length, ending with Chart B before working the final garter-stitch band. Want an even bigger shawl? Use a thicker yarn and the appropriate-sized needle for the yarn.

**Remember:** If using a thicker yarn, you'll need additional yardage when following the pattern as written.

**Row 5:** K3, yo, k2, k2tog, yo, *k8, (k2tog, yo) 4 times; rep from * to last 15 sts, k8, k2tog, yo, k2, yo, k3.

**Row 6:** K3, yo, k1, p4, k8, *p8, k8; rep from * to last 8 sts, p4, k1, yo, k3.

**Row 7:** K3, yo, k2, (k2tog, yo) twice, *k8, (k2tog, yo) 4 times; rep from * to last 17 sts, k8, (k2tog, yo) twice, k2, yo, k3.

**Row 8:** K3, yo, k1, p6, k8, *p8, k8; rep from * to last 10 sts, p6, k1, yo, k3.

## Written Instructions for Chart B

*Depending on what you prefer, follow either the chart or the written instructions below.*

**Row 1 (RS):** K3, yo, *k8, (yo, ssk) 4 times; rep from * to last 11 sts, k8, yo, k3.

**Row 2 (WS):** K3, yo, k9, *p8, k8; rep from * to last 4 sts, k1, yo, k3.

**Row 3:** K3, yo, k2, *k8, (yo, ssk) 4 times; rep from * to last 13 sts, k10, yo, k3.

**Row 4:** K3, yo, k1, p2, k8, *p8, k8; rep from * to last 6 sts, p2, k1, yo, k3.

**Row 5:** K3, yo, k2, yo, ssk, *k8, (yo, ssk) 4 times; rep from * to last 15 sts, k8, yo, ssk, k2, yo, k3.

**Row 6:** K3, yo, k1, p4, k8, *p8, k8; rep from * to last 8 sts, p4, k1, yo, k3.

**Row 7:** K3, yo, k2, (yo, ssk) twice, *k8, (yo, ssk) 4 times; rep from * to last 17 sts, k8, (yo, ssk) twice, k2, yo, k3.

**Row 8:** K3, yo, k1, p6, k8, *p8, k8; rep from * to last 10 sts, p6, k1, yo, k3.

## FINISHING

BO loosely kwise on RS. Block shawl to finished measurements given at beg of patt. With tapestry needle

### GARNETT CHART A

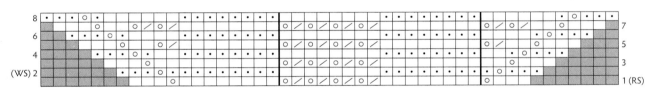

Repeat = 16 sts

#### LEGEND

☐ K on RS, P on WS    ╱ K2tog
· P on RS, K on WS    ▨ No stitch
○ YO

### GARNETT CHART B

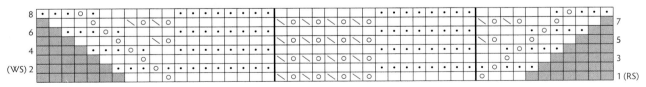

Repeat = 16 sts

#### LEGEND

☐ K on RS, P on WS    ╲ Ssk
· P on RS, K on WS    ▨ No stitch
○ YO

# Over the Moon

Wrap yourself in this warm alpaca-blend shawl on a moonlit walk. Stroll through the neighborhood with your partner or sneak into the woods looking for werewolves— you're bound to turn heads with this one.

## FINISHED MEASUREMENTS

- 56" wide × 26" deep (142.2 × 60cm)

## MATERIALS

- 450 yds (411.5m) fingering-weight yarn
- US Size 4 (3.5mm) circular needle, 32" (81.3cm) cable or longer, or size required for gauge
- 4 stitch markers
- Tapestry needle
- Blocking supplies

## YARN INFORMATION

- Sample uses 1 skein of Alpaca Sox from Classic Elite Yarns (60% alpaca/20% merino/20% nylon; 3.5oz/100g; 450 yds/411.5m) in color 1807 Verdis

## GAUGE

- 22 sts and 32 rows = 4" (10.2cm) in St st, blocked
- *Gauge is not critical for this pattern; however, a different gauge will affect the finished size of the project as well as the amount of yarn needed.*

## PATTERN NOTES

- If using additional stitch markers to mark each stitch repeat, on some rows, the stitch markers will need to be rearranged. For this pattern, you'll need to rearrange these stitch markers on Rows 5, 7, and 9 of Chart A, Row 9 of Chart C, and Rows 7, 9, 11, and 13 of Chart D. For more information on this technique, see page 14.

**The geometric elements of the lace pattern add a touch of structure and whimsy to this top-down triangle shawl.**

## INSTRUCTIONS

Work garter-tab CO as follows:

CO 3 sts. Knit 6 rows. Turn work 90-degrees clockwise, and pick up and knit 3 sts along the left edge. Turn work 90-degrees clockwise, and pick up and knit 3 sts from CO edge—9 sts total.

**Row 1 (RS):** K3, pm, yo, k1, yo, pm, k1 (center st), pm, yo, k1, yo, pm, k3—13 sts.

**Row 2 (WS):** K3, purl to last 3 sts, k3.

**Row 3:** K3, sm, yo, knit to next marker, yo, sm, k1, sm, yo, knit to last 3 sts, yo, sm, k3—17 sts.

Work Rows 2 and 3 another 3 times—29 sts.

Rep Row 2 once more.

## BODY OF SHAWL

Work Charts A, B, and C four times total—285 sts.

*Note: Charts are worked A, B, C, A, B, C, etc.*

### Written Instructions for Chart A

*Depending on what you prefer, follow either the chart or the written instructions below.*

**Row 1 (RS):** K3, yo, *k1, k2tog, yo, k1, yo, ssk, k2; rep from * to 3 sts before center st, k3, yo, k1, yo, k3, **k2, k2tog, yo, k1, yo, ssk, k1; rep from ** to last 3 sts, yo, k3.

**Row 2 and all even-numbered rows (WS):** K3, purl to last 3 sts, k3.

**Row 3:** K3, yo, k1, *k2tog, yo, k3, yo, ssk, k1; rep from * to 4 sts before center st, k4, yo, k1, yo, k4, **k1, k2tog, yo, k3, yo, ssk; rep from ** to last 4 sts, k1, yo, k3.

**Row 5:** K3, yo, k1, k2tog, *yo, k5, yo, sk2p; rep from * to 4 sts before center st, yo, k4, yo, k1, yo, k4, yo, **sk2p, yo, k5, yo; rep from ** to last 6 sts, ssk, k1, yo, k3.

**Row 7:** K3, yo, k2, k2tog, *yo, k5, yo, CDD; rep from * to 5 sts before center st, yo, k5, yo, k1, yo, k5, yo, **CDD, yo, k5, yo; rep from ** to last 7 sts, ssk, k2, yo, k3.

### STITCH COUNTS FOR BODY OF SHAWL

| | |
|---|---|
| First rep of Charts A, B, and C | 93 sts |
| Second rep of Charts A, B, and C | 157 sts |
| Third rep of Charts A, B, and C | 221 sts |
| Fourth rep of Charts A, B, and C | 285 sts |

# Make It Bigger!

If you have a second skein of yarn, add additional repeats of Charts A, B, and C before moving on to Chart D.

**Row 9:** K3, yo, k3, k2tog, *yo, k5, yo, CDD; rep from * to 6 sts before center st, yo, k6, yo, k1, yo, k6, yo, **CDD, yo, k5, yo; rep from ** to last 8 sts, ssk, k3, yo, k3.

**Row 10:** K3, purl to last 3 sts, k3.

## Written Instructions for Chart B

*Depending on what you prefer, follow either the chart or the written instructions below.*

**Row 1 (RS):** K3, yo, k1, k2tog, yo, k2, *k1, yo, ssk, k1, k2tog, yo, k2; rep from * to center st, yo, k1, yo, **k2, yo, ssk, k1, k2tog, yo, k1; rep from ** to last 8 sts, k2, yo, ssk, k1, yo, k3.

**Row 2 and all even-numbered rows (WS):** K3, purl to last 3 sts, k3.

**Row 3:** K3, yo, k1, k2tog, yo, k3, *k2, yo, sk2p, yo, k3; rep from * to 1 st before center st, (k1, yo) twice, k1, **k3, yo, sk2p, yo, k2; rep from ** to last 9 sts, k3, yo, ssk, k1, yo, k3.

**Row 5:** K3, yo, k4, k2tog, yo, k1, *yo, ssk, k3, k2tog, yo, k1; rep from * to 2 sts before center st, k2, yo, k1, yo, k2, **k1, yo, ssk, k3, k2tog, yo; rep from ** to last 10 sts, k1, yo, ssk, k4, yo, k3.

**Row 7:** K3, yo, k1, yo, ssk, k1, k2tog, yo, k2, *k1, yo, ssk, k1, k2tog, yo, k2; rep from * to 3 sts before center st, k3, yo, k1, yo, k3, **k2, yo, ssk, k1, k2tog, yo, k1; rep from ** to last 11 sts, k2, yo, ssk, k1, k2tog, yo, k1, yo, k3.

**Row 8:** K3, purl to last 3 sts, k3.

## Written Instructions for Chart C

*Depending on what you prefer, follow either the chart or the written instructions below.*

**Row 1 (RS):** K3, yo, k1, *k2, yo, sk2p, yo, k3; rep from * to 4 sts before center st, k4, yo, k1, yo, k4, **k3, yo, sk2p, yo, k2; rep from ** to last 4 sts, k1, yo, k3.

**Row 2 and all even numbered rows (WS):** K3, purl to last 3 sts, k3.

**Row 3:** K3, yo, k2, *k2, yo, CDD, yo, k3; rep from * to 5 sts before center st, k5, yo, k1, yo, k5, **k3, yo, CDD, yo, k2; rep from ** to last 5 sts, k2, yo, k3.

**Row 5:** K3, yo, k3, *k2, yo, CDD, yo, k3; rep from * to 6 sts before center st, k2, yo, k2tog, yo, k2, yo, k1, yo, k2, yo, ssk, yo, k2, **k3, yo, CDD, yo, k2; rep from ** to last 6 sts, k3, yo, k3.

**Row 7:** K3, yo, k1, yo, k2tog, yo, k1, *k2tog, yo, k3, yo, ssk, k1; rep from * to 8 sts before center st, k2tog, yo, k3, yo, ssk, (k1, yo) twice, k1, k2tog, yo, k3, yo, ssk, **k1, k2tog, yo, k3, yo, ssk; rep from ** to last 7 sts, k1, yo, ssk, yo, k1, yo, k3.

**Row 9:** K3, yo, k1, yo, k2tog, yo, k1, yo, sk2p, *yo, k5, yo, sk2p; rep from * to 8 sts before center st, yo, k1, yo, k2tog, yo, k1, yo, ssk, k2, yo, k1, yo, k2, k2tog, yo, k1, yo, ssk, yo, k1, yo, **sk2p, yo, k5, yo; rep from ** to last 10 sts, sk2p, yo, k1, yo, ssk, yo, k1, yo, k3.

**Row 10:** K3, purl to last 3 sts, k3.

## LACE EDGING

Work Rows 1–13 of Chart D—317 sts.

## Written Instructions for Chart D

*Depending on what you prefer, follow either the chart or the written instructions below.*

**Row 1 (RS):** K3, yo, *k1, k2tog, yo, k1, yo, ssk, k2; rep from * to 3 sts before center st, k3, yo, k1, yo, k3, **k2, k2tog, yo, k1, yo, ssk, k1; rep from ** to last 3 sts, yo, k3.

**Row 2 and all even-numbered rows (WS):** K3, purl to last 3 sts, k3.

**Row 3:** K3, yo, k1, *k2tog, yo, k3, yo, ssk, k1; rep from * to 4 sts before center st, k4, yo, k1, yo, k4, **k1, k2tog, yo, k3, yo, ssk; rep from ** to last 4 sts, k1, yo, k3.

**Row 5:** K3, yo, k1, k2tog, *yo, k1, yo, sk2p; rep from * to 4 sts before center st, yo, k4, yo, k1, yo, k4, yo, **sk2p, yo, k1, yo; rep from ** to last 6 sts, ssk, k1, yo, k3.

**Row 7:** K3, yo, k2, k2tog, *yo, k1, yo, CDD; rep from * to 5 sts before center st, yo, k1, yo, ssk, yo, k2, yo, k1, yo, k2, yo, k2tog, yo, k1, yo, **CDD, yo, k1, yo; rep from ** to last 7 sts, ssk, k2, yo, k3.

**Row 9:** K3, yo, k3, k2tog, *yo, k1, yo, CDD; rep from * to 3 sts before center st, yo, k3, yo, k1, yo, k3, yo, **CDD, yo, k1, yo; rep from ** to last 8 sts, ssk, k3, yo, k3.

**Row 11:** K3, yo, k4, k2tog, *yo, k1, yo, CDD; rep from * to 4 sts before center st, yo, k4, yo, k1, yo, k4, yo, **CDD, yo, k1, yo; rep from ** to last 9 sts, ssk, k4, yo, k3.

**Row 13:** K3, yo, k2, yo, k2tog, yo, k1, k2tog, *yo, k1, yo, CDD; rep from * to 5 sts before center st, yo, k5, yo, k1, yo, k5, yo, **CDD, yo, k1, yo; rep from ** to last 10 sts, ssk, k1, yo, ssk, yo, k2, yo, k3.

**Row 14:** K3, purl to last 3 sts, k3.

## FINISHING

BO loosely kwise on RS. Block shawl to finished measurements given at beg of patt. With tapestry needle, weave in ends.

## OVER THE MOON CHART A

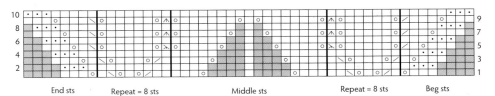

End sts      Repeat = 8 sts      Middle sts      Repeat = 8 sts      Beg sts

**LEGEND**

- ☐ K on RS, P on WS
- ☐○ YO
- SK2P
- • P on RS, K on WS
- ∧ CDD
- ∕ K2tog
- ∖ Ssk
- ▨ No stitch

## OVER THE MOON CHART B

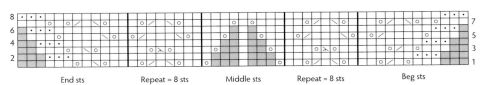

End sts      Repeat = 8 sts      Middle sts      Repeat = 8 sts      Beg sts

## OVER THE MOON CHART C

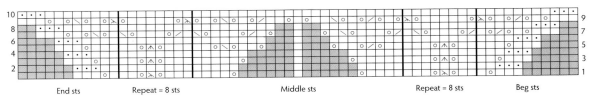

End sts      Repeat = 8 sts      Middle sts      Repeat = 8 sts      Beg sts

## OVER THE MOON CHART D

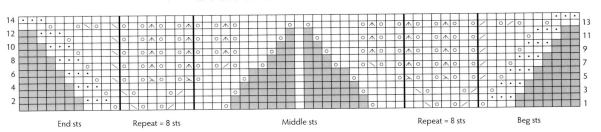

End sts      Repeat = 8 sts      Middle sts      Repeat = 8 sts      Beg sts

# Waveland

This shawl starts at the top center and is worked outward in garter stitch. After the body of the shawl is complete, additional stitches are cast on to work the lace border perpendicularly to the body—a fun, quick knit!

## FINISHED MEASUREMENTS
- 54" wide × 14" deep (137.2 × 35.6cm)

## MATERIALS
- 400 yds (365.8m) fingering-weight yarn
- US Size 5 (3.75mm) circular needle, 32" (81.3cm) cable or longer, or size required for gauge
- Tapestry needle
- Blocking supplies

## YARN INFORMATION
- Sample uses 1 skein of Entice MCN from Hazel Knits (70% superwash merino/20% cashmere/10% nylon; 4oz/114g; 400 yds/365.8m) in color In the Clover

## GAUGE
- 20 sts and 24 rows = 4" (10.2cm) in garter st, blocked
- *Gauge is not critical for this pattern; however, a different gauge will affect the finished size of the project as well as the amount of yarn needed.*

**With a lace edge pattern that's so easy, no chart is necessary.**

## INSTRUCTIONS

Work garter-tab CO as follows:

CO 3 sts. Knit 8 rows. Turn work 90-degrees clockwise, and pick up and knit 4 sts along the left edge. Turn work 90-degrees clockwise, and pick up and knit 3 sts from CO edge—10 sts total.

## BODY OF SHAWL

**Row 1 (RS):** K2, yo, k1, yo, k4, yo, k1, yo, k2—14 sts.

**Row 2 (WS):** Knit all sts.

**Row 3:** K2, (yo, k1) 3 times, yo, k4, yo, (k1, yo) 3 times, k2—22 sts.

**Row 4:** Knit all sts.

**Row 5:** K2, yo, k1, yo, knit to last 3 sts, yo, k1, yo, k2—4 sts inc; 26 sts.

Work Rows 4 and 5 another 50 times—226 sts.

Work Row 4 once more.

## LACE EDGING

Using the knitted cast on, CO 15 sts.

**Row 1 (RS):** K14, ssk last border st with first body st on left needle, turn.

**Row 2 (WS):** Sl1 wyib, k14, turn.

Work Rows 1 and 2 once more.

**Row 3:** K3, (k2tog, yo) 4 times, k3, ssk last border st with first body st on left needle, turn.

**Row 4:** Sl1 wyib, k14, turn.

**Row 5:** K4, (k2tog, yo) 4 times, k2, ssk last border st with first body st on left needle, turn.

**Row 6:** Sl1 wyib, k14, turn.

Work Rows 3–6 another 110 times—2 sts from body of shawl remain unworked.

**Row 7:** K14, ssk last border st with first body st on left needle, turn.

**Row 8:** Sl1 wyib, k14, turn.

Work Rows 7 and 8 once more.

## FINISHING

BO loosely kwise on RS. Block shawl to finished measurements given at beg of patt. With tapestry needle, weave in ends.

# Timberline

Worked from the bottom up, this short-row shawl is quick to knit and fun to wear. A vertical lace pattern with paired decreases adds texture to the bottom of the piece.

## FINISHED MEASUREMENTS
- 52" wide × 15" deep (132.1 × 38.1cm)

## MATERIALS
- 600 yds (548.6m) worsted-weight yarn
- US Size 8 (5.0mm) circular needle, 32" (81.3cm) cable or longer, or size required for gauge
- Tapestry needle
- Blocking supplies

## YARN INFORMATION
- Sample uses 3 skeins of For Better or Worsted from Anzula Luxury Fibers (80% superwash merino/10% cashmere/10% nylon; 4oz/114g; 200 yds/182.9m) in color Bark

## GAUGE
- 14 sts and 28 rows = 4" (10.2cm) in St st, blocked
- *Gauge is not critical for this pattern; however, a different gauge will affect the finished size of the project as well as the amount of yarn needed.*

**The vertical lace pattern reminds me of walking along a nearby park trail and coming to the edge of the woods lined with big, beautiful trees.**

# INSTRUCTIONS

CO 253 sts.

Using the chart or written instructions, work Chart A twice (32 rows).

Work Chart B once (16 rows)—181 sts.

**Row 1 (RS):** K95, turn work (86 sts unworked).

**Row 2 (WS):** P9, turn work (86 sts unworked).

**Row 3:** K8, ssk, k3, turn work (82 sts unworked)—180 sts total.

**Row 4:** P11, p2tog, p3, turn work (82 sts unworked)—179 sts total.

**Row 5:** Knit to 1 st before gap (1 st before previous turning point), ssk, k3, turn work.

**Row 6:** Purl to 1 st before gap (1 st before previous turning point), p2tog, p3, turn work.

Rep Rows 5 and 6 another 19 times (2 sts unworked on each end)—139 sts total.

**Next Row (RS):** Knit to 1 st before gap (1 st before previous turning point), ssk, k1—138 sts.

Rep last row on WS—137 sts.

Knit 6 rows.

## Written Instructions for Chart A

*Depending on what you prefer, follow either the chart or the written instructions below.*

**Rows 1, 3, 5, 7, 9, 11, and 13 (RS):** K2, yo, ssk, *k2tog, yo, k3, yo, ssk; rep from * to last 4 sts, k2tog, yo, k2.

**Rows 2, 4, 6, 8, 10, and 12 (WS):** K2, purl to the last 2 sts, k2.

**Rows 14–16:** Knit all sts.

Rep Rows 1–16 for patt.

## Written Instructions for Chart B

*Depending on what you prefer, follow either the chart or the written instructions below.*

**Rows 1, 3, 5, 7, 9, and 11 (RS):** K2, yo, ssk, *k2tog, yo, k3, yo, ssk; rep from * to last 4 sts, k2tog, yo, k2.

**Rows 2, 4, 6, 8, 10, and 12 (WS):** K2, purl to the last 2 sts, K2.

**Row 13:** K2, ssk, *K2tog, K3, ssk; rep from * to last 4 sts, K2tog, K2.

**Rows 14–16:** Knit all sts.

# Make It Your Own!

Chart A can be repeated as many times as you like before moving on to Chart B. This shawl would also look stunning in a bulky-weight yarn! Just remember that adding chart repeats or changing yarns will affect the amount of yarn needed.

# FINISHING

BO loosely kwise on RS. Block shawl to finished measurements given at beg of patt. With tapestry needle, weave in ends.

## TIMBERLINE CHART A

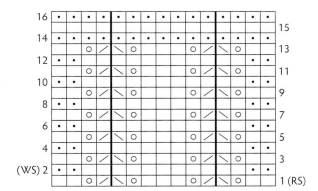

Repeat = 7 sts

### LEGEND

☐ K on RS, P on WS

• P on RS, K on WS

○ YO

╱ K2tog

╲ Ssk

## TIMBERLINE CHART B

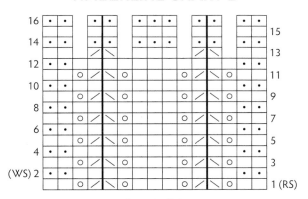

Repeat = 7 sts

### LEGEND

☐ K on RS, P on WS

• P on RS, K on WS

○ YO

╱ K2tog

╲ Ssk

# Francolin

The kite-like lace motif makes me want to wear this shawl outside on a windy morning to see where it might take me. This shawl is going to make you take flight!

## FINISHED MEASUREMENTS

- 60" wide × 28" deep (152.4 × 71.1cm)

## MATERIALS

- 485 yds (443.5m) fingering-weight yarn
- US Size 5 (3.75mm) circular needle, 32" (81.3cm) cable or longer, or size required for gauge
- 4 stitch markers
- Tapestry needle
- Blocking supplies

## YARN INFORMATION

- Sample uses 2 skeins of Spud & Chloë Fine Sock from Blue Sky Alpacas (80% superwash wool/20% silk; 2.3oz/65g; 248 yds/226.8m) in color 7814 Shitake

## GAUGE

- 16 sts and 22 rows = 4" (10.2cm) in St st, blocked
- *Gauge is not critical for this pattern; however, a different gauge will affect the finished size of the project as well as the amount of yarn needed.*

## PATTERN NOTES

- If using additional stitch markers to mark each stitch repeat, on some rows, the stitch markers will need to be rearranged. For this pattern, you'll need to rearrange these stitch markers on Row 11 of Chart A and Row 7 of Chart B. For more information on this technique, see page 14.

**An allover lace motif in a soft, drapey yarn makes this cozy wrap whimsical and versatile.**

## INSTRUCTIONS

Work garter-tab CO as follows:

CO 3 sts. Knit 6 rows. Turn work 90-degrees clockwise, and pick up and knit 3 sts along the left edge. Turn work 90-degrees clockwise, and pick up and knit 3 sts from CO edge—9 sts total.

**Row 1 (RS):** K3, pm, yo, k1, yo, pm, k1 (center st), pm, yo, k1, yo, pm, k3—13 sts.

**Row 2 (WS):** K3, purl to last 3 sts, k3.

**Row 3:** K3, sm, yo, knit to next marker, yo, sm, k1, sm, yo, knit to last 3 sts, yo, sm, k3—17 sts.

Work Rows 2 and 3 twice more—25 sts.

Rep Row 2 once more.

## BODY OF SHAWL

Continue working first 3 sts and last 3 sts in garter st (knit every row) and working the center st in St st (knit on RS, purl on WS).

Using the chart or written instructions for chart, work Chart A between st markers on each half of shawl 3 times total—217 sts.

Using the chart or written instructions for chart, work Chart B between st markers on each half of shawl twice—281 sts.

| STITCH COUNTS FOR BODY OF SHAWL | |
|---|---|
| First rep of Chart A | 89 sts |
| Second rep of Chart A | 153 sts |
| Third rep of Chart A | 217 sts |
| First rep of Chart B | 249 sts |
| Second rep of Chart B | 281 sts |

### Written Instructions for Chart A

*Depending on what you prefer, follow either the chart or the written instructions below.*

**Row 1 (RS):** Yo, *k3, yo, sk2p, yo, k2; rep from * to 1 st before marker, k1, yo.

**Row 2 and all even-numbered rows (WS):** Purl all sts.

**Row 3:** Yo, k1, *k3, yo, sk2p, yo, k2; rep from * to 2 sts before marker, k2, yo.

**Row 5:** Yo, k2, *k3, yo, sk2p, yo, k2; rep from * to 3 sts before marker, k3, yo.

**Row 7:** Yo, k3, *k2, k2tog, yo, k1, yo, ssk, k1; rep from * to 4 sts before marker, k4, yo.

**Row 9:** Yo, k2, yo, ssk, *k1, k2tog, yo, k3, yo, ssk; rep from * to 5 sts before marker, k1, k2tog, yo, k2, yo.

**Row 11:** Yo, k1, yo, k2tog, yo, k1, yo, *sk2p, yo, k5, yo; rep from * to 7 sts before marker, sk2p, yo, k1, yo, ssk, yo, k1, yo.

**Row 13:** Yo, ssk, yo, k3, yo, k2tog, *k1, ssk, yo, k3, yo, k2tog; rep from * to 8 sts before marker, k1, ssk, yo, k3, yo, k2tog, yo.

**Row 15:** Yo, k2, yo, ssk, yo, k1, yo, k2tog, k1, *k2, ssk, yo, k1, yo, k2tog, k1; rep from * to 9 sts before marker, k2, ssk, yo, k1, yo, k2tog, yo, k2, yo.

**Row 17:** Yo, k2, yo, k2tog, yo, k1, yo, sk2p, yo, k2, *k3, yo, sk2p, yo, k2; rep from * to 11 sts before marker, k3, yo, sk2p, yo, k1, yo, ssk, yo, k2, yo.

**Row 19:** Yo, k4, yo, k2tog, yo, k1, yo, sk2p, yo, k2, *k3, yo, sk2p, yo, k2; rep from * to 13 sts before marker, k3, yo, sk2p, yo, k1, yo, ssk, yo, k4, yo.

**Row 21:** Yo, k2, yo, k2tog, yo, k2, *k3, yo, sk2p, yo, k2; rep from * to 7 sts before marker, k3, yo, ssk, yo, k2, yo.

**Row 22:** Purl all sts.

Rep Rows 1–22 for patt.

## Written Instructions for Chart B

*Depending on what you prefer, follow either the chart or the written instructions below.*

**Row 1 (RS):** Yo, *k3, yo, sk2p, yo, k2; rep from * to 1 st before marker, k1, yo.

**Row 2 and all even-numbered rows (WS):** Purl all sts.

**Row 3:** Yo, k1, *k2, k2tog, yo, k1, yo, ssk, k1; rep from * to 2 sts before marker, k2, yo.

**Row 5:** Yo, k2, *k1, k2tog, yo, k3, yo, ssk; rep from * to 3 sts before marker, k3, yo.

**Row 7:** Yo, k2, yo, *sk2p, yo, k5, yo; rep from * to 5 sts before marker, sk2p, yo, k2, yo.

**Row 9:** (Yo, k1) twice, yo, k2tog, *k1, ssk, yo, k3, yo, k2tog; rep from * to 5 sts before marker, k1, ssk, (yo, k1) twice, yo.

**Row 11:** Yo, k2, yo, k1, yo, k2tog, k1, *k2, ssk, yo, k1, yo, k2tog, k1; rep from * to 7 sts before marker, k2, ssk, yo, k1, yo, k2, yo.

**Row 12:** Purl all sts.

Rep Rows 1–12 for patt.

## LACE EDGING

Using the chart or written instructions for chart, work Chart C between st markers on each half of shawl—313 sts.

## Written Instructions for Chart C

*Depending on what you prefer, follow either the chart or the written instructions below.*

**Row 1 (RS):** Yo, *k1, yo, k2, sk2p, yo, k2; rep from * to 1 st before marker, k1, yo.

**Row 2 and all even-numbered rows (WS):** Purl all sts.

**Row 3:** Yo, k1, *yo, k3, sk2p, k1, yo, k1; rep from * to 2 sts before marker, k2, yo.

**Row 5:** Yo, k2, *k3, yo, sk2p, k2, yo; rep from * to 3 sts before marker, k3, yo.

**Row 7:** Yo, k3, *yo, k1, yo, k1, sk2p, k3; rep from * to 4 sts before marker, k4, yo.

**Row 9:** Yo, k2tog, yo, k2, *k1, yo, k2, sk2p, yo, k2; rep from * to 5 sts before marker, k1, yo, k2, k2tog, yo.

**Row 11:** Yo, k1, k2tog, k1, yo, k1, *yo, k3, sk2p, k1, yo, k1; rep from * to 6 sts before marker, yo, k3, k2tog, k1, yo.

**Row 13:** Yo, k1, yo, sk2p, k2, yo, *k3, yo, sk2p, k2, yo; rep from * to 7 sts before marker, k3, yo, k2tog, k2, yo.

**Row 15:** (Yo, k1) twice, k2tog, k3, *(yo, k1) twice, sk2p, k3; rep from * to 8 sts before marker, (yo, k1) twice, sk2p, k3, yo.

**Row 16:** Purl all sts.

## FINISHING

BO loosely kwise on RS. Block shawl to finished measurements given at beg of patt. With tapestry needle, weave in ends.

# Make It Bigger!

There are lots of options to make this shawl larger if you have extra yarn. Any of the charts can be repeated to add length to your shawl.

## FRANCOLIN CHART A

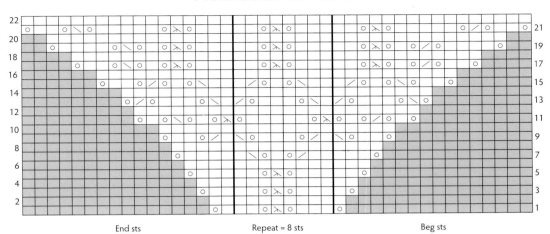

End sts · Repeat = 8 sts · Beg sts

## FRANCOLIN CHART B

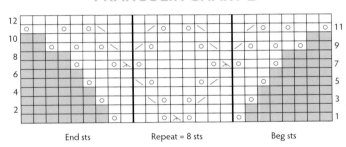

End sts · Repeat = 8 sts · Beg sts

## FRANCOLIN CHART C

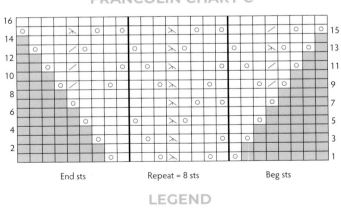

End sts · Repeat = 8 sts · Beg sts

## LEGEND

| | |
|---|---|
| ⊙ YO | ╱ K2tog |
| ☐ K on RS, P on WS | ╲ Ssk |
| ⋋ SK2P | ▨ No stitch |

# Demeter

Half-pi (semicircle) shawls are perfect for someone wanting a cozy shawl. The shape allows for excellent drape, hanging on your shoulders like a cape. Simple lace patterns and easy increases make this pattern an excellent choice if you're trying this shawl shape for the first time.

## FINISHED MEASUREMENTS
- 54" wide × 29" deep (137.2 × 73.7cm)

## MATERIALS
- 840 yds (768.1m) fingering-weight yarn
- US Size 4 (3.5mm) circular needle, 32" (81.3cm) cable or longer, or size required for gauge
- Tapestry needle
- Blocking supplies

## YARN INFORMATION
- Sample uses 2 skeins of Breathless from Shalimar Yarns (75% superwash merino/15% cashmere/10% silk; 3.5oz/100g; 420 yds) in the color Limerick

## GAUGE
- 24 sts and 28 rows = 4" (10.2cm) in St st, blocked
- *Gauge is not critical for this pattern; however, a different gauge will affect the finished size of the project as well as the amount of yarn needed.*

## PATTERN NOTES
- If using stitch markers to mark each stitch repeat, on some rows, the stitch markers will need to be rearranged. For this pattern, for Chart B the markers will move on Row 7. For Chart C, the markers will move on Rows 1 and 3. For Chart D, the markers will be moved on Row 1. For more information on this technique, see page 14.

**The semicircular shape of this allover lace pattern is fun to knit and easy to wear.**

## INSTRUCTIONS

Work garter-tab CO as follows:
CO 3 sts. Knit 6 rows. Turn work 90-degrees clockwise, and pick up and knit 3 sts along the left edge. Turn work 90-degrees clockwise, and pick up and knit 3 sts from CO edge—9 sts total.
**Next Row (WS):** Knit all sts.

## SECTION 1 (4 ROWS)

**Inc Row (RS):** (K1, yo) to last st, k1—17 sts.
Knit 3 rows.

## SECTION 2 (8 ROWS)

**Inc Row (RS):** (K1, yo) to last st, k1—33 sts.
**Row 2 (WS):** K2, purl to last 2 sts, k2.
**Row 3:** Knit all sts.
Work Rows 2 and 3 twice more.
Rep Row 2 once more.

## SECTION 3 (18 ROWS)

**Inc Row (RS):** (K1, yo) to last st, k1—65 sts.
**Next Row (WS):** K2, yo, purl to last 2 sts, yo, k2—67 sts.
Using the chart or the written instructions for the chart, work Chart A 4 times.

## Written Instructions for Chart A

*Depending on what you prefer, follow either the chart or the written instructions below.*
**Row 1 (RS):** K4, k2tog, yo, *k1, yo, ssk, k1, k2tog, yo; rep from * to last 7 sts, k1, yo, ssk, k4.
**Row 2 (WS):** K2, purl to last 2 sts, k2.
**Row 3:** K3, k2tog, yo, k1, *k2, yo, sk2p, yo, k1; rep from * to last 7 sts, k2, yo, ssk, k3.
**Rows 4:** K2, purl to last 2 sts, k2.

## SECTION 4 (34 ROWS)

**Inc Row (RS):** (K1, yo) to last st, k1—133 sts.
**Next Row (WS):** K2, purl to last 2 sts, k2.
Using the chart or the written instructions for the chart, work Chart B 4 times.

## Written Instructions for Chart B

*Depending on what you prefer, follow either the chart or the written instructions below.*
**Row 1 (RS):** K4, k2tog, yo, *k1, yo, ssk, k1, k2tog, yo; rep from * to last 7 sts, k1, yo, ssk, k4.
**Row 2 and all even-numbered rows (WS):** K2, purl to last 2 sts, k2.
**Row 3:** K3, k2tog, k1, yo, *k1, yo, k1, sk2p, k1, yo; rep from * to last 7 sts, k1, yo, k1, ssk, k3.
**Row 5:** K4, yo, ssk, *k1, k2tog, yo, k1, yo, ssk; rep from * to last 7 sts, k1, k2tog, yo, k4.
**Row 7:** K4, yo, k1, *sk2p, (k1, yo) twice, k1; rep from * to last 8 sts, sk2p, k1, yo, k4.
**Row 8:** K2, purl to last 2 sts, k2.

## SECTION 5 (109 ROWS)

**Inc row (RS):** (K1, yo) to last st, k1—265 sts.
**Next Row (WS):** K2, purl to last 2 sts, k2.
Using the chart or the written instructions for the chart, work Chart C 4 times (48 rows).
Using the chart or the written instructions for the chart, work Chart D 14 times (56 rows).
Work Rows 1–3 of Chart D once more.

## Written Instructions for Chart C

*Depending on what you prefer, follow either the chart or the written instructions below.*
**Row 1 (RS):** K2, *k3, yo, sk2p, yo; rep from * to last 5 sts, k5.
**Row 2 and all even-numbered rows (WS):** K2, purl to last 2 sts, k2.
**Row 3:** Rep Row 1.
**Row 5:** Knit all sts.
**Row 7:** K2, *yo, sk2p, yo, k3; rep from * to last 5 sts, yo, sk2p, yo, k2.
**Row 9:** Rep Row 7.
**Row 11:** Knit all sts.
**Row 12:** K2, purl to last 2 sts, k2.

## Written Instructions for Chart D

*Depending on what you prefer, follow either the chart or the written instructions below.*

**Row 1 (RS):** K2, *k3, yo, sk2p, yo; rep from * to last 5 sts, k5.

**Row 2 (WS):** K2, purl to last 2 sts, k2.

**Row 3:** K2, *yo, sk2p, yo, k3; rep from * to last 5 sts, yo, sk2p, yo, k2.

**Row 4:** K2, purl to last 2 sts, k2.

## FINISHING

BO loosely pwise on WS. Block shawl to finished measurements given at beg of patt. With tapestry needle, weave in ends.

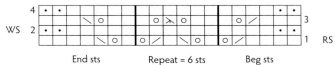

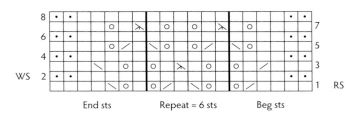

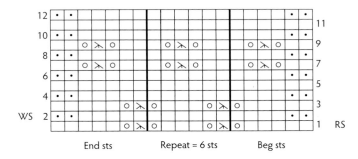

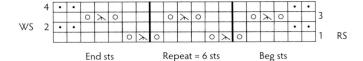

# Lari

This is a simple cowl or infinity scarf with the volume turned up. An increasing lace panel is inserted into a background of stockinette stitch, adding interest and beauty to the project—and your wardrobe!

## SIZES
- Cowl [Infinity Scarf]

## FINISHED MEASUREMENTS
- Circumference: 24" [48"] (61cm) [121.9cm]
- Depth: 6 1/2" (16.5cm)

## MATERIALS
- 150 yds [300 yds] (137.2m) [274.3m] DK-weight yarn
- US Size 6 (4.0mm) circular needle, 32" (81.3cm) cable or longer, or size required for gauge
- Tapestry needle
- Blocking supplies

## YARN INFORMATION
- Sample uses 2 skeins of Lively DK from Hazel Knits (90% superwash merino/10% nylon; 4.6oz/130g; 275 yds/251.5m) in color Tropical Sunset

## GAUGE
- 20 sts and 32 rows = 4" (10.2cm) in St st, blocked
- *Gauge is not critical for this pattern; however, a different gauge will affect the finished size of the project as well as the amount of yarn needed.*

## PATTERN NOTES
- The pattern is written for the cowl, while the instructions for the infinity scarf is written in brackets [ ], where necessary. If only one instruction is given, it should be worked for both sizes. The infinity scarf is shown.
- For this project, three stitch markers are used. You may find it helpful to use two matching markers for the chart and a different stitch marker to mark the beginning of the round.

**An increasing lace panel adds a captivating detail to this otherwise simple project.**

## INSTRUCTIONS

CO 100 [200] sts.

Join in the round, being careful not to twist sts. Pm to mark beg of rnd.

**Ribbing Rnd:** *K1, p1; rep from * to end of rnd.

Rep Ribbing Rnd another 4 times (5 rnds total).

**Set-Up Rnd:** K2, m1, k43 [k93], pm, k9, pm, knit to end of rnd—101 [201] sts.

Work the following rnds while, **at the same time**, working the Chart:

**Rnd 1:** Knit to 2 sts before the marker, k2tog, sm, work row 1 of chart to next marker, sm, ssk, knit to end of rnd.

**Rnd 2:** Knit to marker, sm, work row 2 of chart to marker, sm, knit to end of rnd.

**Rnd 3:** Knit to 2 sts before marker, k2tog, sm, work next row of Chart to marker, sm, ssk, knit to end of rnd.

**Rnd 4:** Knit to marker, sm, work next row of chart to marker, sm, knit to end of rnd.

Rep Rnds 3 and 4 another 21 times, working next subsequent rnd of Chart each rnd—55 sts total in between markers for chart.

**Next Rnd:** K2, k2tog, knit to marker, remove marker, knit to next marker, remove marker, knit to end of rnd—100 [200] sts.

Work Ribbing Rnd for 5 rnds.

### Written Instructions for Chart

*Depending on what you prefer, follow either the chart or the written instructions below.*

**Rnds 1, 3, and 5:** Yo, knit to marker, yo.

**Rnds 2, 4, and 6:** Knit all sts.

**Rnd 7:** Yo, k3, *k2, k2tog, yo, k1, yo, ssk, k1; rep from * to 4 sts before marker, k4, yo.

**Rnd 8:** K4, *k1, k2tog, yo, k3, yo, ssk; rep from * to 5 sts before marker, k5.

**Rnds 9, 11, and 13:** Yo, knit to marker, yo.

**Rnds 10, 12, and 14:** Knit all sts.

**Rnd 15:** Yo, k1, k2tog, yo, k1, yo, ssk, k1, *k2, k2tog, yo, k1, yo, ssk, k1; rep from * to marker, yo.

**Rnd 16:** *K1, k2tog, yo, k3, yo, ssk; rep from * to 1 st before marker, k1.

Rep Rows 1–16 for patt.

# Make It Your Own!

Want a deeper cowl? Keep repeating Rounds 3 and 4, working the next subsequent round of the chart to your desired depth, ending with Round 6 or 14. Work the remainder of the pattern as written. Adding rounds to your cowl or infinity scarf will increase the amount of yarn needed to complete the project.

# FINISHING

BO loosely in patt. Block cowl to finished measurements given at beg of patt. With tapestry needle, weave in ends.

## LARI CHART

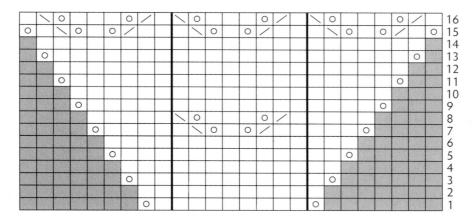

Repeat = 8 sts

## LEGEND

| | | | |
|---|---|---|---|
| ☐ K | ╱ K2tog | ▨ No stitch | |
| ⊙ YO | ╲ Ssk | | |

# Potrero Hill Shawl

This sophisticated semicircular shawl is a perfect showcase for seed stitch and lace. Using traditional pi-shawl math, you can make this shawl as big as you want. Notes on how to enlarge it are included in the pattern.

## FINISHED MEASUREMENTS

- 60" wide × 24" deep (152.4 × 61cm)

## MATERIALS

- 740 yds (676.7m) DK-weight yarn
- US Size 6 (4.0mm) circular needle, 32" (81.3cm) cable or longer, or size required for gauge
- Tapestry needle
- Blocking supplies

## YARN INFORMATION

- Sample uses 3 skeins of Breathless DK from Shalimar Yarns (75% superwash merino/15% cashmere/10% silk; 4oz/114g; 270 yds/246.9m) in color Bing

## GAUGE

- 18 sts and 24 rows = 4" (10.2cm) in St st, blocked
- *Gauge is not critical for this pattern; however, a different gauge will affect the finished size of the project as well as the amount of yarn needed.*

**The zigzag pattern that emerges in this knit gives a modern feel.**

## INSTRUCTIONS

Work garter-tab CO as follows:

CO 2 sts. Knit 20 rows. Turn work 90-degrees clockwise, and pick up and knit 3 sts along the left edge. Turn work 90-degrees clockwise, and pick up and knit 2 sts from CO edge—14 sts total.

**Set-Up Row (WS):** Knit all sts.

**Row 1 (RS):** K2, (yo, k1) to last 2 sts, k2—24 sts.

**Row 2:** K2, purl to last 2 sts, k2.

**Row 3:** Knit all sts.

**Row 4:** Rep Row 2.

## BODY OF SHAWL

**Inc Row (RS):** K2, (yo, k1) to last 2 sts, k2—44 sts.

**Row 2 (WS):** K2, purl to last 2 sts, k2.

**Row 3:** Knit all sts.

Rep Rows 2 and 3 another 3 times. Rep Row 2 once more.

Work Inc Row—84 sts.

**Next Row (WS):** K2, purl to last 2 sts, k2.

Using the chart or the written instructions for the chart, work Chart A once.

Work Inc Row—164 sts.

**Next Row (WS):** K2, purl to last 2 sts, k2.

Using the chart or the written instructions for the chart, work Chart B once.

Work Inc Row—324 sts.

**Next Row (WS):** K2, purl to last 2 sts, k2.

Using the chart or the written instructions for the chart, work Chart B twice.

Work Rows 1–14 of Chart B once more.

## Written Instructions for Chart A

*Depending on what you prefer, follow either the chart or the written instructions below.*

**Row 1 (RS):** K2, *k6, (yo, k2tog) twice; rep from * to last 2 sts, k2.

**Row 2 (WS):** K2, *k1, p9; rep from * to last 2 sts, k2.

**Row 3:** K2, *k5, (yo, k2tog) twice, k1; rep from * to last 2 sts, k2.

**Row 4:** Rep Row 2.

**Row 5:** K2, *k4, (yo, k2tog) twice, p1, k1; rep from * to last 2 sts, k2.

**Row 6:** K2, *k1, p1, k1, p7; rep from * to last 2 sts, k2.

**Row 7:** K2, *k3, (yo, k2tog) twice, k1, p1, k1; rep from * to last 2 sts, k2.

**Row 8:** Rep Row 6.

**Row 9:** K2, *k2, (yo, k2tog) twice, (p1, k1) twice; rep from * to last 2 sts, k2.

**Row 10:** K2, *(k1, p1) twice, k1, p5; rep from * to last 2 sts, k2.

**Row 11:** K2, *k1 (yo, k2tog) twice, (k1, p1) twice, k1; rep from * to last 2 sts, k2.

**Row 12:** Rep Row 10.

**Row 13:** K2, *(yo, k2tog) twice, (p1, k1) 3 times; rep from * to last 2 sts, k2.

**Row 14:** Rep Row 10.

# Make It Your Own!

For an even larger shawl, work the increase row again (644 stitches) and continue working Chart B to the desired length, ending with Row 14 or 28. Remember: Adjusting the size will affect the amount of yarn you'll need.

## Written Instructions for Chart B

*Depending on what you prefer, follow either the chart or the written instructions below.*

**Row 1 (RS):** K2, *(ssk, yo) twice, k6; rep from * to last 2 sts, k2.

**Row 2 (WS):** K2, *p9, k1; rep from * to last 2 sts, k2.

**Row 3:** K2, *k1, (ssk, yo) twice, k5; rep from * to last 2 sts, k2.

**Row 4:** Rep Row 2.

**Row 5:** K2, *k1, p1, (ssk, yo) twice, k4; rep from * to last 2 sts, k2.

**Row 6:** K2, *p7, k1, p1, k1; rep from * to last 2 sts, k2.

**Row 7:** K2, *k1 p1, k1, (ssk, yo) twice, k3; rep from * to last 2 sts, k2.

**Row 8:** Rep Row 6.

**Row 9:** K2, *(k1 p1) twice, (ssk, yo) twice, k2; rep from * to last 2 sts, k2.

**Row 10:** K2, *p5, (k1, p1) twice, k1; rep from * to last 2 sts, k2.

**Row 11:** K2, *(k1, p1) twice, k1, (ssk, yo) twice, k1; rep from * to last 2 sts, k2.

**Row 12:** Rep Row 10.

**Row 13:** K2, *(k1, p1) 3 times, (ssk, yo) twice; rep from * to last 2 sts, k2.

**Row 14:** Rep Row 10.

**Row 15:** K2, *k6, (yo, k2tog) twice; rep from * to last 2 sts, k2.

**Row 16:** K2, *k1, p9; rep from * to last 2 sts, k2.

**Row 17:** K2, *k5, (yo, k2tog) twice, k1; rep from * to last 2 sts, k2.

**Row 18:** Rep Row 16.

**Row 19:** K2, *k4, (yo, k2tog) twice, p1, k1; rep from * to last 2 sts, k2.

**Row 20:** K2, *k1, p1, k1, p7; rep from * to last 2 sts, k2.

**Row 21:** K2, *k3, (yo, k2tog) twice, k1, p1, k1; rep from * to last 2 sts, k2.

**Row 22:** Rep Row 20.

**Row 23:** K2, *k2, (yo, k2tog) twice, (p1, k1) twice; rep from * to last 2 sts, k2.

**Row 24:** K2, *(k1, p1) twice, k1, p5; rep from * to last 2 sts, k2.

**Row 25:** K2, *k1 (yo, k2tog) twice, (k1, p1) twice, k1; rep from * to last 2 sts, k2.

**Row 26:** Rep Row 24.

**Row 27:** K2, *(yo, k2tog) twice, (p1, k1) 3 times; rep from * to last 2 sts, k2.

**Row 28:** Rep Row 24.

## FINISHING

BO loosely kwise on RS. Block shawl to finished measurements given at beg of patt. With tapestry needle, weave in ends.

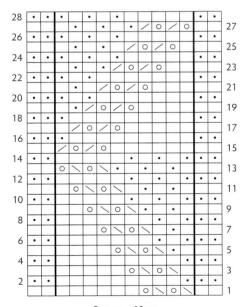

Repeat = 10 sts

### LEGEND

☐ K on RS, P on WS    ╱ K2tog

• P on RS, K on WS    ╲ SSK

○ YO

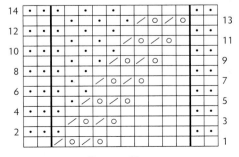

Repeat = 10 sts

# Potrero Hill Stole

For this stunning showpiece stole, use a smooth yarn that shows off the stitch pattern. Like all the other scarves and stoles in this book, you can make this stole any size you like.

## FINISHED MEASUREMENTS
- 68" × 14" (172.7 × 35.6cm), before seaming

## MATERIALS
- 820 yds (749.8m) fingering-weight yarn
- US Size 5 (3.75mm) circular needle, 32" (81.3cm) cable or longer, or size required for gauge
- Tapestry needle
- Blocking supplies

## YARN INFORMATION
- Sample uses 2 skeins of Breathless from Shalimar Yarns (75% superwash merino/15% cashmere/10% silk; 3.5oz/100g; 420 yds/384m) in color Black Truffle

## GAUGE
- 20 sts and 32 rows = 4" (10.2cm) in St st, blocked
- *Gauge is not critical for this pattern; however, a different gauge will affect the finished size of the project as well as the amount of yarn needed.*

**The generous dimensions of the stole combined with the open stitch pattern make it cozy yet lightweight.**

## INSTRUCTIONS

CO 64 sts.

**Next Row (WS):** Knit all sts.

Using the chart or written instructions for chart, work Chart until piece measures approximately 64" (162.6cm) from CO edge, ending with Row 27.

**Final Row (WS):** Knit all sts.

## Written Instructions for Chart

*Depending on what you prefer, follow either the chart or the written instructions below.*

**Row 1 (RS):** K2, *(ssk, yo) twice, k6; rep from * to last 2 sts, k2.

**Row 2 (WS):** K2, *p9, k1; rep from * to last 2 sts, k2.

**Row 3:** K2, *k1, (ssk, yo) twice, k5; rep from * to last 2 sts, k2.

**Row 4:** Rep Row 2.

**Row 5:** K2, *k1, p1, (ssk, yo) twice, k4; rep from * to last 2 sts, k2.

**Row 6:** K2, *p7, k1, p1, k1; rep from * to last 2 sts, k2.

**Row 7:** K2, *k1 p1, k1, (ssk, yo) twice, k3; rep from * to last 2 sts, k2.

**Row 8:** Rep Row 6.

**Row 9:** K2, *(k1 p1) twice, (ssk, yo) twice, k2; rep from * to last 2 sts, k2.

**Row 10:** K2, *p5, (k1, p1) twice, k1; rep from * to last 2 sts, k2.

**Row 11:** K2, *(k1, p1) twice, k1, (ssk, yo) twice, k1; rep from * to last 2 sts, k2.

**Row 12:** Rep Row 10.

**Row 13:** K2, *(k1, p1) 3 times, (ssk, yo) twice; rep from * to last 2 sts, k2.

**Row 14:** Rep Row 10.

**Row 15:** K2, *k6, (yo, k2tog) twice; rep from * to last 2 sts, k2.

**Row 16:** K2, *k1, p9; rep from * to last 2 sts, k2.

**Row 17:** K2, *k5, (yo, k2tog) twice, k1; rep from * to last 2 sts, k2.

**Row 18:** Rep Row 16.

**Row 19:** K2, *k4, (yo, k2tog) twice, p1, k1; rep from * to last 2 sts, k2.

**Row 20:** K2, *k1, p1, k1, p7; rep from * to last 2 sts, k2.

**Row 21:** K2, *k3, (yo, k2tog) twice, k1, p1, k1; rep from * to last 2 sts, k2.

# Make It Your Own!

If you'd like to make a smaller scarf, cast on 34 stitches. As long as you cast on a multiple of 10, plus 4 stitches, the scarf can be any size you like.

**Row 22:** Rep Row 20.

**Row 23:** K2, *k2, (yo, k2tog) twice, (p1, k1) twice; rep from * to last 2 sts, k2.

**Row 24:** K2, *(k1, p1) twice, k1, p5; rep from * to last 2 sts, k2.

**Row 25:** K2, *k1, (yo, k2tog) twice, (k1, p1) twice, k1; rep from * to last 2 sts, k2.

**Row 26:** Rep Row 24.

**Row 27:** K2, *(yo, k2tog) twice, (p1, k1) 3 times; rep from * to last 2 sts, k2.

**Row 28:** Rep Row 24.

Rep Rows 1–28 for patt.

## FINISHING

BO loosely kwise on RS. Block shawl to finished measurements given at beg of patt. With tapestry needle, weave in ends.

### POTRERO HILL STOLE CHART

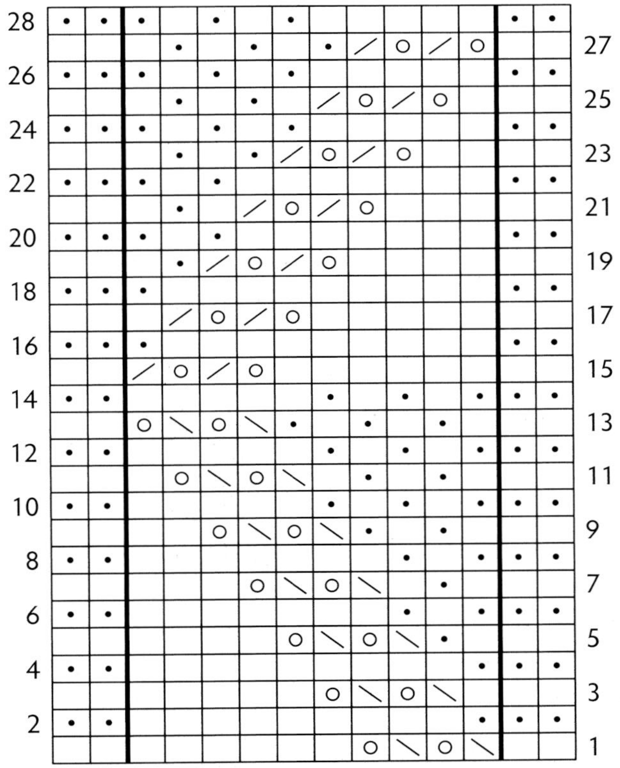


Repeat = 10 sts

### LEGEND

- [ ] K on RS, P on WS
- [•] P on RS, K on WS
- [O] YO
- [/] K2tog
- [\] SSK

# Lycopod

A delicate top-down triangle shawl, Lycopod is the perfect warm weather piece. It can easily be made larger or smaller, depending on the knitter's mood.

## FINISHED MEASUREMENTS
- 84" wide × 41" deep (213.4 × 104.1cm)

## MATERIALS
- 790 yds (722.4m) fingering-weight yarn
- US Size 4 (3.5mm) circular needle, 32" (81.3cm) cable or longer, or size required for gauge
- 4 stitch markers
- Tapestry needle
- Blocking supplies

## YARN INFORMATION
- Sample uses 2 skeins of Tosh Sock from Madelintosh (100% superwash merino wool; 3.5oz/100g; 395 yds/361.2m) in color Cousteau

## GAUGE
- 20 sts and 24 rows = 4" (10.2cm) in St st, blocked
- *Gauge is not critical for this pattern; however, a different gauge will affect the finished size of the project as well as the amount of yarn needed.*

## PATTERN NOTES
- Charts for this pattern show RS rows only. See Instructions for how to work WS rows.
- If using additional stitch markers to mark each stitch repeat, on some rows, the stitch markers will need to be rearranged. For this pattern, you'll need to rearrange these stitch markers on Rows 5, 9, and 13 of Chart B, and Rows 9, 11, 13, 19, and 21 for Chart C. For more information on this technique, see page 14.

**If you love to knit lace, you'll love knitting this shawl.**

## INSTRUCTIONS

Work garter-tab CO as follows:

CO 3 sts. Knit 6 rows. Turn work 90-degrees clockwise, and pick up and knit 3 sts along the left edge. Turn work 90-degrees clockwise, and pick up and knit 3 sts from CO edge—9 sts total.

**Set-Up Row (WS):** K3, pm, p1, pm, p1 (this is the center st), pm, p1, pm, k3.

## BODY OF SHAWL

**Row 1 (RS):** K3, sm, work Row 1 of Chart A, sm, k1, sm, work Row 1 of Chart A, sm, k3.

**Row 2 and all even-numbered rows (WS):** K3, purl to last 3 sts slipping the markers along the way, k3.

Continue in established pattern, working first 3 sts and last 3 sts in garter st (knit every row) and the center st in St st (knit on RS, purl on WS). On all WS rows, work Row 2 of Body of Shawl (above). On RS rows, work charts on each half of shawl as follows (starting with Row 3 of Chart A):

Chart A—41 sts.

Chart B—105 sts.

Chart C–169 sts.

Chart B—233 sts.

Chart C—297 sts.

Chart B—361 sts.

Chart C—425 sts.

Do not work final WS row.

### Written Instructions for Chart A

*Depending on what you prefer, follow either the chart or the written instructions below.*

**Row 1 (RS):** Yo, k1, yo.

**Row 3:** Yo, k3, yo.

**Row 5:** Yo, k5, yo.

**Row 7:** Yo, k2, yo, sk2p, yo, k2, yo.

**Row 9:** Yo, k2, k2tog, yo, k1, yo, ssk, k2, yo.

**Row 11:** Yo, k2, k2tog, yo, k3, yo, ssk, k2, yo.

**Row 13:** Yo, k2, (k2tog, yo) twice, k1, (yo, ssk) twice, k2, yo.

**Row 15:** Yo, k2, (k2tog, yo) twice, k3, (yo, ssk) twice, k2, yo.

# Make It Bigger [or Smaller]!

With extra [less] yarn, you can add [remove] as many repeats of Charts B and C as you like.

## Written Instructions for Chart B

*Depending on what you prefer, follow either the chart or the written instructions below.*

**Row 1 (RS):** Yo, k1, *k1, (k2tog, yo) 3 times, k1, (yo, ssk) 3 times, k2; rep from * to marker, yo.

**Row 3:** Yo, k2, *(k2tog, yo) 3 times, k3, (yo, ssk) 3 times, k1; rep from * to last st before marker, k1, yo.

**Row 5:** Yo, k1, yo, sk2p, *yo, (k2tog, yo) twice, k5, (yo, ssk) twice, yo, sk2p; rep from * to last st before marker, yo, k1, yo.

**Row 7:** Yo, k4, *(k2tog, yo) twice, k7, (yo, ssk) twice, k1; rep from * to 3 sts before marker, k3, yo.

**Row 9:** Yo, k1, yo, ssk, yo, sk2p, *yo, k2tog, yo, k1, yo, k2, sk2p, k2, yo, k1, yo, ssk, yo, sk2p; rep from * to last 3 sts before marker, yo, k2tog, yo, k1, yo.

**Row 11:** Yo, k6, *k2tog, yo, k3, yo, k1, sk2p, k1, yo, k3, yo, ssk, k1; rep from * to last 5 sts before marker, k5, yo.

**Row 13:** *Yo, k5, yo, sk2p; rep from * to last 5 sts before marker, yo, k5, yo.

**Row 15:** Yo, k8, *k1, yo, k1, sk2p, k1, yo, k3, yo, k1, sk2p, k1, yo, k2; rep from * to last 7 sts before marker, k7, yo.

**Row 17:** Yo, k2, yo, k4, k2tog, yo, k1, *yo, ssk, yo, sk2p, yo, k5, yo, sk2p, yo, k2tog, yo, k1; rep from * to last 8 sts before marker, yo, ssk, k4, yo, k2, yo.

**Row 19:** Yo, (k1, yo) twice, ssk, k3, k2tog, yo, k2, *k1, (yo, ssk) twice, yo, k1, sk2p, k1, yo, (k2tog, yo) twice, k2; rep from * to last 10 sts before marker, k1, yo, ssk, k3, k2tog, (yo, k1) twice, yo.

**Row 21:** Yo, k2, yo, k1, (yo, ssk) twice, k1, (k2tog, yo) twice, k1, *(yo, ssk) 3 times, yo, sk2p, yo, (k2tog, yo) 3 times, k1; rep from * to last 12 sts before marker, (yo, ssk) twice, k1, (k2tog, yo) twice, k1, yo, k2, yo.

**Row 23:** Yo, k1, k2tog, yo, k3, yo, ssk, yo, sk2p, yo, k2tog, yo, k2, *k1, (yo, ssk) 3 times, k1, (k2tog, yo) 3 times, k2; rep from * to last 14 sts before marker, k1, yo, ssk, yo, sk2p, yo, k2tog, yo, k3, yo, ssk, yo, k1, yo.

## Written Instructions for Chart C

*Depending on what you prefer, follow either the chart or the written instructions below.*

**Row 1 (RS):** Yo, k1, *(yo, ssk) 3 times, yo, sk2p, yo, (k2tog, yo) 3 times, k1; rep from * to marker, yo.

**Row 3:** Yo, k2, *k1, (yo, ssk) 3 times, k1, (k2tog, yo) 3 times, k2; rep from * to last st before marker, k1, yo.

**Row 5:** Yo, k3, *k2, (yo, ssk) twice, yo, sk2p, yo, (k2tog, yo) twice, k3; rep from * to last 2 sts before marker, k2, yo.

**Row 7:** Yo, k4, *k3, (yo, ssk) twice, k1, (k2tog, yo) twice, k4; rep from * to last 3 sts before marker, k3, yo.

**Row 9:** Yo, k1, yo, k2, sk2p, *k2, yo, k1, yo, ssk, yo, sk2p, yo, k2tog, yo, k1, yo, k2, sk2p; rep from * to last 3 sts before marker, k2, yo, k1, yo.

**Row 11:** Yo, k3, yo, k1, sk2p, *k1, yo, k3, yo, ssk, k1, k2tog, yo, k3, yo, k1, sk2p; rep from * to last 4 sts before marker, k1, yo, k3, yo.

**Row 13:** *Yo, k5, yo, sk2p; rep from * to last 5 sts before marker, yo, k5, yo.

**Row 15:** Yo, k8, *k1, yo, k1, sk2p, k1, yo, k3, yo, k1, sk2p, k1, yo, k2; rep from * to 7 sts before marker, k7, yo.

**Row 17:** Yo, k2, yo, k7, *k2, yo, sk2p, yo, k2tog, yo, k1, yo, ssk, yo, sk2p, yo, k3; rep from * to last 8 sts before marker, k6, yo, k2, yo.

**Row 19:** Yo, k1, yo, k3, (yo, ssk) twice, yo, k1, sk2p, *k1, yo, (k2tog, yo) twice, k3, (yo, ssk) twice, yo, k1, sk2p; rep from * to last 9 sts before marker, k1, yo, (k2tog, yo) twice, k3, yo, k1, yo.

**Row 21:** Yo, k2, yo, k3, (yo, ssk) 3 times, yo, sk2p, *yo, (k2tog, yo) 3 times, k1, (yo, ssk) 3 times, yo, sk2p; rep from * to last 11 sts before marker, yo, (k2tog, yo) 3 times, k3, yo, k2, yo.

**Row 23:** Yo, k1, yo, k2tog, yo, k5, (yo, ssk) 3 times, k1, *(k2tog, yo) 3 times, k3, (yo, ssk) 3 times, k1; rep from * to last 14 sts before marker, (k2tog, yo) 3 times, k5, yo, ssk, yo, k1, yo.

## FINISHING

BO loosely pwise on WS. Block shawl to finished measurements given at beg of patt. With tapestry needle, weave in ends.

## LYCOPOD CHART A

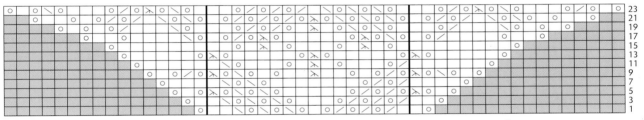

End sts          Beg sts

## LEGEND

| | | | |
|---|---|---|---|
| ☐ | K on RS, P on WS | ◹ | K2tog |
| • | P on RS, K on WS | ⋊ | Sk2p |
| ◺ | Ssk | ▨ | No stitch |
| ⊙ | YO | | |

## LYCOPOD CHART B

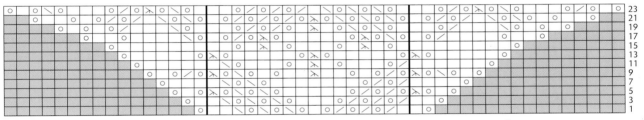

End sts          Repeat = 16 sts          Beg sts

## LYCOPOD CHART C

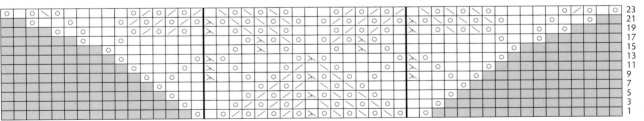

End sts          Repeat = 16 sts          Beg sts

# Flower Garden

Spring has sprung all over this shawlette. Floral panels run down the edges and center. Little flowers at the bottom of the shawl will keep you dreaming of springtime.

## FINISHED MEASUREMENTS

- 42" wide × 17" deep (106.7 × 43.2cm)

## MATERIALS

- 500 yds (457.2m) fingering-weight yarn
- US Size 3 (3.25mm) circular needle, 32" (81.3cm) cable or longer, or size required for gauge
- 6 stitch markers
- Tapestry needle
- Blocking supplies

## YARN INFORMATION

- Sample uses 2 skeins of Sock-a-licious from Kolláge Yarns (70% fine superwash merino/20% nylon/10% mulberry silk; 3.5oz/100g; 354 yds/323.7m) in color 7813 Sangria

## GAUGE

- 22 sts and 32 rows = 4" (10.2cm) in St st, blocked
- *Gauge is not critical for this pattern; however, a different gauge will affect the finished size of the project as well as the amount of yarn needed.*

**This pattern introduces a lace design on the edges and center, offering interest from all angles.**

## INSTRUCTIONS

CO 63 sts.

Knit 3 rows.

**Row 1 (RS):** K2, *pm, k17, pm, k4; rep from * once, pm, k17, pm, k2.

**Row 2 (WS):** K2, purl to last 2 sts (slipping markers), K2.

## BODY OF SHAWL

**Row 1 (RS):** K2, *sm, work row 1 of Chart A, sm, yo, knit to next marker, yo; rep from * once more, sm, work Row 1 of Chart A, sm, k2—67 sts.

**Row 2 (WS):** K2, purl to last 2 sts (slipping markers), k2.

**Row 3:** K2, *sm, work next RS row of Chart A, sm, yo, knit to next marker, yo; rep from * once more, sm, work next RS row of Chart A, sm, k2.

**Row 4:** K2, purl to last 2 sts (slipping markers), k2.

Continue in established pattern, working Rows 3 and 4 above, while **at the same time** working next odd-numbered (RS) row of Chart A on RS rows until chart has been worked a total of 4 times—255 sts.

Continue in established pattern, working through Row 11 of Chart A—279 sts.

Work Row 4 above once more.

## LACE EDGING

**Row 1 (RS):** K2, *sm, work next RS row of Chart A, sm, work Row 1 of Chart B; rep from * once, sm, work next RS row of Chart A, sm, k2.

**Row 2 (WS):** K2, purl to last 2 sts (slipping markers), k2.

**Row 3:** K2, *sm, work next RS row of Chart A, sm, work next RS row of Chart B; rep from * once, sm, work next RS row of Chart A, sm, k2.

**Row 4:** K2, purl to last 2 sts (slipping markers), k2.

Work Rows 3 and 4 another 3 times—299 sts.

Work Row 3 once more—303 sts.

Knit 1 row on WS.

### Written Instructions for Chart A

*Depending on what you prefer, follow either the chart or the written instructions below.*

**Row 1 (RS):** K7, yo, sk2p, yo, k7.

**Row 2 and all even-numbered rows (WS):** Purl all sts.

**Row 3:** K6, yo, k2tog, k1, ssk, yo, k6.

**Row 5:** K5, yo, k2tog, k3, ssk, yo, k5.

**Row 7:** K4, yo, k2tog, k5, ssk, yo, k4.

**Row 9:** K4, ssk, yo, k5, yo, k2tog, k4.

**Row 11:** K5, ssk, yo, k3, yo, k2tog, k5.

**Row 13:** K2, (ssk, yo) 3 times, k1, (yo, k2tog) 3 times, k2.

**Row 15:** K3, (ssk, yo) 3 times, k1, (yo, k2tog) twice, k3.

**Row 17:** K4, (ssk, yo) twice, k1, (yo, k2tog) twice, k4.

**Row 19:** K5, (ssk, yo) twice, k1, yo, k2tog, k5.

**Row 21:** K6, ssk, yo, k1, yo, k2tog, k6.

**Row 23:** K7, ssk, yo, k8.

## Written Instructions for Chart B

*Depending on what you prefer, follow either the chart or the written instructions below.*

**Row 1 (RS):** Yo, *k2, yo, k3tog, yo, k3; rep from * to marker, yo.

**Row 2 and all even-numbered rows (WS):** Purl all sts.

**Row 3:** Yo, k1, *ssk, yo, k3, yo, k2tog, k1; rep from * to 1 st before marker, k1, yo.

**Row 5:** Yo, k2, *k2, yo, k3tog, yo, k3; rep from * to 2 sts before marker, k2, yo.

**Row 7:** Yo, k3, *yo, ssk, yo, sk2p, yo, k2tog, yo, k1; rep from * to 3 sts before marker, k3, yo.

**Row 9:** Yo, k4, *k2, yo, sk2p, yo, k3; rep from * to 4 sts before marker, k4, yo.

**Row 11:** Yo, k5, *k2, yo, sk2p, yo, k3; rep from * to 5 sts before marker, k5, yo.

## FINISHING

BO loosely pwise on RS. Block shawl to finished measurements given at beg of patt. With tapestry needle, weave in ends.

### FLOWER GARDEN CHART A

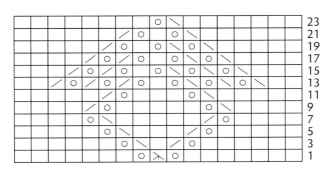

Worked over 17 sts

### FLOWER GARDEN CHART B

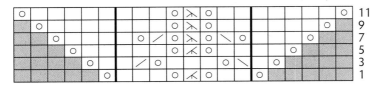

End sts          Repeat = 8 sts          Beg sts

Only RS rows are charted. Purl all sts on WS rows.

### LEGEND

| | | | |
|---|---|---|---|
| ⊡ | YO | ╱ | K2tog |
| ☐ | K on RS | ⋉ | SK2P |
| ⋌ | K3tog | ▨ | No stitch |
| ╲ | Ssk | | |

# Sparrow

Start with a circular pi shawl construction, and then transition into increases typically seen in triangular shawls. The combination creates a shawl that will drape beautifully over your shoulders.

**The lace transitions from a simple to a more complex pattern.**

## FINISHED MEASUREMENTS
- 52" wide × 24" deep (132.1 × 61cm)

## MATERIALS
- 800 yds (731.5m) fingering-weight yarn
- US Size 4 (3.5mm) circular needle, 32" (81.3cm) cable or longer, or size required for gauge
- 6 stitch markers
- Tapestry needle
- Blocking supplies

## YARN INFORMATION
- Sample uses 2 skeins of Entice MCN from Hazel Knits (70% superwash merino/20% cashmere/10% nylon; 4oz/114g; 400 yds/365.8m) in color Lichen

## GAUGE
- 20 sts and 24 rows = 4" (10.2cm) in St st, blocked
- *Gauge is not critical for this pattern; however, a different gauge will affect the finished size of the project as well as the amount of yarn needed.*

## PATTERN NOTES
- If using additional stitch markers to mark each stitch repeat, on some rows, the stitch markers will need to be rearranged. For this pattern, you'll need to rearrange these markers on Rows 7, 9, 11, and 13 of Chart B. For Chart C, the markers will need to be rearranged on Rows 1, 5, 11, 13, 15, and 17. For more information on this technique, see page 14.

## INSTRUCTIONS

Work garter-tab CO as follows:

CO 2 sts. Knit 18 rows. Turn work 90-degrees clockwise, and pick up and knit 9 sts along the left edge. Turn work 90-degrees clockwise, and pick up and knit 2 sts from CO edge—13 sts total.

**Set-Up Row (WS):** K2, p9, k2.

**Inc Row (RS):** K2, (yo, k1) to last 2 sts, yo, k2—23 sts.

**Row 2:** K2, purl to last 2 sts, k2.

**Row 3:** Knit all sts.

**Row 4:** Rep Row 2.

Work Inc Row once more—43 sts.

Work Rows 2 and 3 another 3 times.

Rep Row 2 once more.

Work Inc Row once more—83 sts.

Rep Rows 2 and 3 another 7 times.

Rep Row 2 once more.

Work Inc Row once more—163 sts.

Knit 3 rows.

**Next Row (RS):** K2, pm, k51, pm, k1, pm, k55, pm, k1, pm, k51, pm, k2.

**Next Row (WS):** K2, sm, k2, kfb, knit to next marker, sm, k1, sm, k2, k2tog, k25, k2tog, knit to 4 sts before next marker, k2tog, k2, sm, k1, sm, knit to 3 sts before next marker, kfb, k2, sm, k2—162 sts.

**Next Row:** Knit all sts.

**Next Row:** K2, purl to last 2 sts, k2.

## BODY OF SHAWL

Continue working first 2 sts and last 2 sts in garter st (knit every row).

Work spine sts (i.e., stitches with marker on either side) in St st (knit on RS, purl on WS).

In between markers (starting with 52 sts following set-up rows), work charts in following order:

Using the chart or the written instructions for the chart, work Chart A 4 times—258 sts.Using the chart or the written instructions for the chart, work Chart B once—306 sts.

Using the chart or the written instructions for the chart, work Chart C once—354 sts.

Using the chart or the written instructions for the chart, Chart B once—402 sts.

Work Rows 1–11 of Chart C—438 sts.

# Make It Bigger!

Repeat Charts B and C as desired, ending with Chart B before moving on to final 11 rows of Chart C. Make sure you have an extra skein of yarn or two!

## Written Instructions for Chart A

*Depending on what you prefer, follow either the chart or the written instructions below.*

**Row 1 (RS):** Yo, k2, *k3, yo, ssk, k3; rep from * to 2 sts before marker, k2, yo.

**Row 2 and all even-numbered rows (WS):** Purl all sts.

**Row 3:** Yo, k3, *k2, (yo, ssk) twice, k2; rep from * to 3 sts before marker, k3, yo.

**Row 5:** Yo, k4, *k3, yo, ssk, k3; rep from * to 4 sts before marker, k4, yo.

**Row 7:** Yo, knit to marker, yo.

**Row 8:** Purl all sts.

Rep Rows 1–8 for patt.

## Written Instructions for Chart B

*Depending on what you prefer, follow either the chart or the written instructions below.*

**Row 1 (RS):** Yo, k2, *k3, yo, ssk, k3; rep from * to 2 sts before marker, k2, yo.

**Row 2 and all even-numbered rows (WS):** Purl all sts.

**Row 3:** Yo, k3, *k1, k2tog, yo, k1, yo, ssk, k2; rep from * to 3 sts before marker, k3, yo.

**Row 5:** Yo, k4, *(k2tog, yo) twice, k1, yo, ssk, k1; rep from * to 4 sts before marker, k4, yo.

**Row 7:** Yo, k3, yo, sk2p, *yo, k2tog, yo, k1, yo, ssk, yo, sk2p; rep from * to 4 sts before marker, yo, k4, yo.

**Row 9:** Yo, k3, yo, ssk, yo, *sk2p, yo, k3, yo, ssk, yo; rep from * to 7 sts before marker, sk2p, yo, k4, yo.

**Row 11:** Yo, k5, yo, sk2p, *yo, k5, yo, sk2p; rep from * to 6 sts before marker, yo, k6, yo.

**Row 13:** Yo, k2tog, k1, yo, ssk, k2, yo, *ssk, k2, yo; rep from * to 9 sts before marker, ssk, k2, yo, ssk, k1, ssk, yo.

**Row 15:** Yo, k2, (yo, ssk) twice, k2, *k2, (yo, ssk) twice, k2; rep from * to 8 sts before marker, k2, (yo, ssk) twice, k2, yo.

**Row 17:** Yo, k4, yo, ssk, k3, *k3, yo, ssk, k3; rep from * to 9 sts before marker, k3, yo, ssk, k4, yo.

**Row 18:** Purl all sts.

| STITCH COUNTS FOR CHART A REPEATS ||
|---|---|
| First rep of Chart A | 186 sts |
| Second rep of Chart A | 210 sts |
| Third rep of Chart A | 234 sts |
| Fourth rep of Chart A | 258 sts |

## Written Instructions for Chart C

*Depending on what you prefer, follow either the chart or the written instructions below.*

**Row 1 (RS):** Yo, k1, yo, *ssk, k6, yo; rep from * to 3 sts before marker, ssk, k1, yo.

**Row 2 and all even-numbered rows (WS):** Purl all sts.

**Row 3:** Yo, k1, yo, ssk, *yo, ssk, k4, yo, ssk; rep from * to last 3 sts before marker, yo, ssk, k1, yo.

**Row 5:** Yo, k3, yo, *ssk, k2, yo; rep from * to last 5 sts before marker, ssk, k3, yo.

**Row 7:** Yo, k1, yo, ssk, k2, *k1, k2tog, yo, k1, yo, ssk, k2; rep from * to last 5 sts before marker, k1, k2tog, yo, k2, yo.

**Row 9:** Yo, k1, (yo, ssk) twice, k1, *k2tog, yo, k1, (yo, ssk) twice, k1; rep from * to last 6 sts before marker, (k2tog, yo) twice, k2, yo.

**Row 11:** Yo, k3, yo, ssk, yo, sk2p, *yo, k2tog, yo, k1, yo, ssk, yo, sk2p; rep from * to last 6 sts before marker, yo, k2tog, yo, k4, yo.

## FINISHING

BO loosely kwise on WS. Block shawl to finished measurements given at beg of patt. With tapestry needle, weave in ends.

## SPARROW CHART A

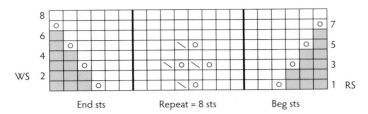

End sts      Repeat = 8 sts      Beg sts

## SPARROW CHART B

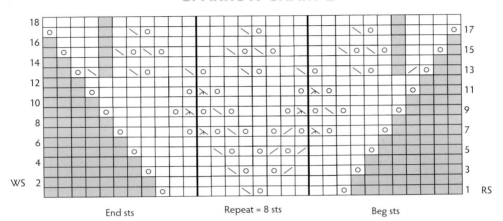

End sts      Repeat = 8 sts      Beg sts

## SPARROW CHART C

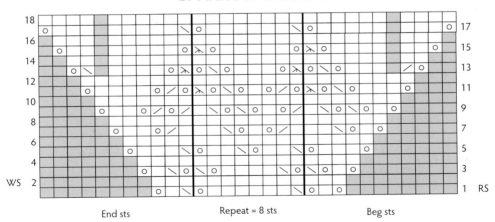

End sts      Repeat = 8 sts      Beg sts

## LEGEND

K on RS, P on WS

• P on RS, K on WS

Ssk

YO

K2tog

Sk2p

No stitch

# Forest Walk

Beautiful lace motifs fall all over this shawl. The center lace panel creates a delicate detail, and a wool-and-silk blend yarn is used to keep the shawl light and airy.

## FINISHED MEASUREMENTS

- 66" wide × 13" deep (167.6 × 33cm)

## MATERIALS

- 435 yds (397.8m) fingering-weight yarn
- US Size 5 (3.75mm) circular needle, 24" (61cm) cable or longer, or size needed to obtain gauge
- 2 stitch markers
- Tapestry needle
- Blocking supplies

## YARN INFORMATION

- Sample uses 1 skein of Silky 435 from JulieSpins (50% silk/50% superwash merino; 3.5oz/100g; 435 yds/397.8m) in the color Lilac

## GAUGE

- 20 sts and 36 rows = 4" (10.2cm) in St st, blocked
- *Gauge is not critical for this pattern; however, a different gauge will affect the finished size of the project as well as the amount of yarn needed.*

## PATTERN NOTES

- If using additional stitch markers to mark each 10-stitch repeat, on some rows, the stitch markers will need to be rearranged. For this pattern, you'll need to rearrange these stitch markers on Row 9 of Chart A and Rows 9 and 11 of Chart B. For more information on this technique, see page 14.

**With a leafy center panel, this shawl is a great accessory for your favorite outdoor activities on a cool spring day.**

The pattern for
the matching
Forest Walk Hat is
on my website.

# INSTRUCTIONS

CO 49 sts.

**Set-Up Row (WS):** K2, (p15, pm) twice, p15, k2.

Work Chart A 6 times—289 sts.

Work Chart B once—315 sts.

## Written Instructions for Chart A

*Depending on what you prefer, follow either the chart or the written instructions below.*

**Row 1 (RS):** K2, yo, k1, *k3, yo, sk2p, yo, k4; rep from * to 4 sts before marker, k2, yo, k2tog, sm, p1, k10, k2tog, yo, k1, p1, sm, ssk, yo, k2, **k4, yo, sk2p, yo, k3; rep from ** to last 3 sts, k1, yo, k2.

**Row 2 (WS):** K3, yo, purl to marker, sm, k1, yo, p2, p2tog, p9, k1, sm, purl to last 3 sts, yo, k3.

**Row 3:** K2, yo, k3, *k2, k2tog, yo, k1, yo, ssk, k3; rep from * to 4 sts before marker, k2, yo,k2tog, sm, p1, k8, k2tog, k1, yo, k2, p1, sm, ssk, yo, k2, **k3, k2tog, yo, k1, yo, ssk, k2; rep from ** to last 5 sts, k3, yo, k2.

**Row 4:** K3, yo, purl to marker, sm, k1, p1, yo, p3, p2tog, p7, k1, sm, purl to last 3 sts, yo, k3.

**Row 5:** K2, yo, k5, *k1, k2tog, yo, k3, yo, ssk, k2; rep from * to 4 sts before marker, k2, yo, k2tog, sm, p1, k6, k2tog, k2, yo, k3, p1, sm, ssk, yo, k2, **k2, k2tog, yo, k3, yo, ssk, k1; rep from ** to last 7 sts, k5, yo, k2.

**Row 6:** K3, yo, purl to marker, sm, k1, p2, yo, p4, p2tog, p5, k1, sm, purl to last 3 sts, yo, k3.

**Row 7:** K2, yo, k4, yo, ssk, k1, *k2tog, yo, k5, yo, ssk, k1; rep from * to 4 sts before marker, k2, yo, k2tog, sm, p1, k4, k2tog, k3, yo, k4, p1, sm, ssk, yo, k2, **k1, k2tog, yo, k5, yo, ssk; rep from ** to last 9 sts, k1, k2tog, yo, k4, yo, k2.

**Row 8:** K3, yo, purl to marker, sm, k1, p3, yo, p5, p2tog, p3, k1, sm, purl to last 3 sts, yo, k3.

**Row 9:** K2, yo, k1, yo, k2tog, yo, k4, yo, sk2p, *yo, k7, yo, sk2p; rep from * to 3 sts before marker, yo, k1, yo, k2tog, sm, p1, k1, yo, ssk, k10, p1, sm, ssk, yo, k1, yo, **sk2p, yo, k7, yo; rep from ** to last 12 sts, sk2p, yo, k4, yo, ssk, yo, k1, yo, k2.

**Row 10:** K3, yo, purl to marker, sm, k1, p9, p2tog tbl, p2, yo, k1, sm, purl to last 3 sts, yo, k3.

**Row 11:** K2, yo, k1, yo, k2tog, yo, k6, k2tog, yo, k1, *yo, ssk, k5, k2tog, yo, k1; rep from * to 4 sts

## STITCH COUNTS FOR SHAWL

| | |
|---|---|
| First rep of Chart A | 89 sts |
| Second rep of Chart A | 129 sts |
| Third rep of Chart A | 169 sts |
| Fourth rep of Chart A | 209 sts |
| Fifth rep of Chart A | 249 sts |
| Sixth rep of Chart A | 289 sts |
| Chart B | 315 sts |

# Make It Your Own!

With a second skein of yarn, you can add as many repeats of Chart A as you like before working Chart B. Remember, changing the number of repeats you work or changing the yarn weight will affect the finished size of your shawl as well as the amount of yarn needed to complete it.

before marker, k2, yo, k2tog, sm, p1, k2, yo, k1, ssk, k8, p1, sm, ssk, yo, k2, **k1, yo, ssk, k5, k2tog, yo; rep from ** to last 14 sts, k1, yo, ssk, k6, yo, ssk, yo, k1, yo, k2.

**Row 12:** K3, yo, purl to marker, sm, k1, p7, p2tog tbl, p3, yo, p1, k1, sm, purl to last 3 sts, yo, k3.

**Row 13:** K2, yo, k1, yo, k2tog, yo, k2, *k1, yo, ssk, k3, k2tog, yo, k2; rep from * to 4 sts before marker, k2, yo, k2tog, sm, p1, k3, yo, k2, ssk, k6, p1, sm, ssk, yo, k2, **k2, yo, ssk, k3, k2tog, yo, k1; rep from ** to last 7 sts, k2, yo, ssk, yo, k1, yo, k2.

**Row 14:** K3, yo, purl to marker, sm, k1, p5, p2tog tbl, p4, yo, p2, k1, sm, purl to last 3 sts, yo, k3.

**Row 15:** K2, yo, k1, yo, k2tog, yo, k5, *k2, yo, ssk, k1, k2tog, yo, k3; rep from * to 4 sts before marker, k2, yo, k2tog, sm, p1, k4, yo, k3, ssk, k4, p1, sm, ssk, yo, k2, **k3, yo, ssk, k1, k2tog, yo, k2; rep from ** to last 10 sts, k5, yo, ssk, yo, k1, yo, k2.

**Row 16:** K3, yo, purl to marker, sm, k1, p3, p2tog tbl, p5, yo, p3, k1, sm, purl to last 3 sts, yo, k3.

Rep Rows 1–16 for patt.

## Written Instructions for Chart B

*Depending on what you prefer, follow either the chart or the written instructions below.*

**Row 1 (RS):** K2, yo, k1, *k3, yo, sk2p, yo, k4; rep from * to 4 sts before marker, k2, yo, k2tog, sm, p1, k10, k2tog, yo, k1, p1, sm, ssk, yo, k2, **k4, yo, sk2p, yo, k3; rep from ** to last 3 sts, k1, yo, k2.

**Row 2 (WS):** K3, yo, purl to marker, sm, k1, yo, p2, p2tog, p9, k1, sm, purl to last 3 sts, yo, k3.

**Row 3:** K2, yo, k3, *k2, k2tog, yo, k1, yo, ssk, k3; rep from * to 4 sts before marker, k2, yo, k2tog, sm, p1, k8, k2tog, k1, yo, k2, p1, sm, ssk, yo, k2, **k3, k2tog, yo, k1, yo, ssk, k2; rep from ** to last 5 sts, k3, yo, k2.

**Row 4:** K3, yo, purl to marker, sm, k1, p1, yo, p3, p2tog, p7, k1, sm, purl to last 3 sts, yo, k3.

**Row 5:** K2, yo, k5, *k1, k2tog, yo, k3, yo, ssk, k2; rep from * to 4 sts before marker, k2, yo, k2tog, sm, p1, k6, k2tog, k2, yo, k3, p1, sm, ssk, yo, k2, **k2, k2tog, yo, k3, yo, ssk, k1; rep from ** to last 7 sts, k5, yo, k2.

**Row 6:** K3, yo, purl to marker, sm, k1, p2, yo, p4, p2tog, p5, k1, sm, purl to last 3 sts, yo, k3.

**Row 7:** K2, yo, k4, yo, ssk, k1, *k2tog, yo, k1, yo, sk2p, yo, k1, yo, ssk, k1; rep from * to 4 sts before marker, k2, yo, k2tog, sm, p1, k4, k2tog, k3, yo, k4, p1, sm, ssk, yo, k2, **k1, k2tog,

yo, k1, yo, sk2p, yo, k1, yo, ssk; rep from ** to last 9 sts, k1, k2tog, yo, k4, yo, k2.

**Row 8:** K3, yo, purl to marker, sm, k1, p3, yo, p5, p2tog, p3, k1, sm, purl to last 3 sts, yo, k3.

**Row 9:** K2, yo, k1, yo, k2tog, yo, k4, yo, sk2p, *yo, k2, yo, sk2p; rep from * to 3 sts before marker, yo, k1, yo, k2tog, sm, p1, k2, k2tog, k4, yo, k5, p1, sm, ssk, yo, k1, yo, **sk2p, yo, k2, yo; rep from ** to last 12 sts, sk2p, yo, k4, yo, ssk, yo, k1, yo, k2.

**Row 10:** K3, yo, purl to marker, sm, k1, p4, yo, p6, p2tog, p1, k1, sm, purl to last 3 sts, yo, k3.

**Row 11:** K2, yo, k1, yo, k2tog, *yo, k2, yo, sk2p; rep from * to 3 sts before marker, yo, k1, yo, k2tog, sm, p1, k2tog, k5, yo, k6, p1, sm, ssk, yo, k1, yo, **sk2p, yo, k2, yo; rep from ** to last 5 sts, ssk, yo, k1, yo, k2.

## FINISHING

BO loosely kwise on WS. Block shawl to finished measurements given at beg of patt. With tapestry needle, weave in ends.

## LEGEND

☐ K on RS, P on WS

• P on RS, K on WS

○ YO

▨ No stitch

╲ Ssk on RS, P2tog tbl on WS

╱ K2tog on RS, P2tog on WS

⋋ Sk2p

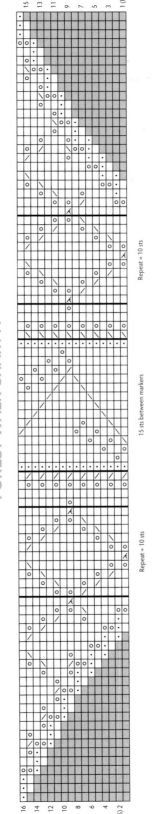

FOREST WALK CHART A

15 sts between markers

Repeat = 10 sts

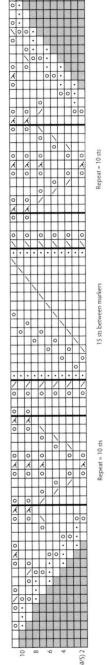

FOREST WALK CHART B

15 sts between markers

Repeat = 10 sts

# Briargate

Sometimes you have two skeins of sock yarn that seem to go perfectly together. Or maybe you had to barely break into a second skein of yarn to finish the toe for a sock. Why not combine them to make a beautiful two-colored shawl?

## FINISHED MEASUREMENTS

- 80" wide × 12 1/2" deep (203.2 × 31.8cm)

## MATERIALS

- 400 yds (365.8m) fingering-weight yarn in Color A
- 400 yds (365.8m) fingering-weight yarn in Color B
- US Size 4 (3.5mm) circular needle, 32" (81.3cm) cable or longer, or size required for gauge
- Tapestry needle
- Blocking supplies

## YARN INFORMATION

- Sample uses Caper Sock from String Theory Hand Dyed Yarn (80% superwash merino/10% cashmere/10% nylon; 4oz/113g; 400 yds/365.8m), in the colors Pewter (Color A—1 skein) and Mallow (Color B—1 skein)

## GAUGE

- 20 sts and 36 rows = 4" (10.2cm) in St st, blocked
- *Gauge is not critical for this pattern; however, a different gauge will affect the finished size of the project as well as the amount of yarn needed.*

**Adding a second color adds interest to this beautiful pattern.**

## BODY OF SHAWL

With Color A, CO 125 sts.

Knit 2 rows.

**Row 1 (RS):** Continue with Color A, k2, yo, knit to last 2 sts, yo, k2—127 sts.

**Row 2 (WS):** K3, yo, purl to last 3 sts, yo, k3—129 sts.

Rep Rows 1 and 2 another 31 times—253 sts.

**Next Row (RS):** K2, yo, knit to last 2 sts, yo, k2—255 sts.

**Next Row (WS):** K3, yo, knit to last 3 sts, yo, k3—257 sts.

Rep last two rows once more—261 sts.

Cut Color A.

## LACE EDGING

With Color B and using the chart or written instructions, work Chart 3 times total.

With Color A, work final edging as follows:

**Row 1 (RS):** K2, yo, knit to last 2 sts, yo, k2—347 sts.

**Row 2 (WS):** K3, yo, knit to last 3 sts, yo, k3—349 sts.

Rep Rows 1 and 2 once more—353 sts.

**Row 3:** K1, *yo twice, sk2p; rep from * to last st, yo twice, k1.

**Row 4:** K1, *(k1, p1) into each yo of double yo, k1; rep from * to last 3 sts, (k1, p1) twice into double yo, k1.

| STITCH COUNTS FOR LACE CHART REPEATS | |
| --- | --- |
| First rep of Chart | 289 sts |
| Second rep of Chart | 317 sts |
| Third rep of Chart | 345 sts |

### Written Instructions for Chart

*Depending on what you prefer, follow either the chart or the written instructions below.*

**Row 1 (RS):** K2, yo, k1, yo, *sk2p, yo, k2tog, yo, k7, yo, ssk, yo; rep from * to last 6 sts, sk2p, yo, k1, yo, k2.

**Row 2 and all even-numbered rows (WS):** K3, yo, purl to last 3 sts, yo, k3.

**Row 3:** K2, yo, k4, *yo, k3tog, yo, k1, yo, k2, sk2p, k2, yo, k1, yo, ssk; rep from * to last 7 sts, yo, k2tog, k3, yo, k2.

**Row 5:** K2, yo, k5, yo, *sk2p, yo, k1, yo, ssk, yo, k1, sk2p, k1, yo, k2tog, yo, k1, yo; rep from * to last 10 sts, k2tog, k6, yo, k2.

**Row 7:** K2, yo, k8, *k4, yo, ssk, yo, sk2p, yo, k2tog, yo, k3; rep from * to last 11 sts, k9, yo, k2.

**Row 9:** K2, yo, k9, yo, *sk2p, k2, yo, k1, yo, ssk, yo, k3tog, yo, k1, yo, k2; rep from * to last 14 sts, sk2p, yo, k9, yo, k2.

**Row 11:** K2, yo, k5, (yo, k2tog, yo, k1) twice, yo, *sk2p, k1, yo, k2tog, yo, k1, yo, sk2p, yo, k1, yo, ssk, yo, k1; rep from * to last 16 sts, sk2p, yo, (k1, yo, k2tog, yo) twice, k5, yo, k2.

**Row 12:** K3, yo, purl to last 3 sts, yo, k3.

Rep Rows 1–12 for patt.

Cut Color B. Color A will be used for remainder of shawl.

# FINISHING

BO loosely kwise on RS. Block shawl to finished measurements given at beg of patt. With tapestry needle, weave in ends.

## BRIARGATE CHART

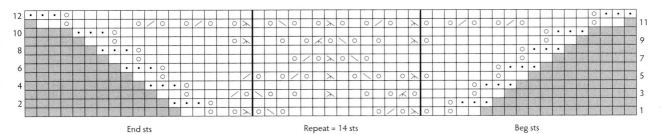

End sts

Repeat = 14 sts

Beg sts

## LEGEND

|  | K on RS, P on WS |  | K2tog |  | K3tog |
|--|--|--|--|--|--|
|  | YO |  | Ssk |  | No stitch |
|  | SK2P |  | P on RS, K on WS |  |  |

# Earth and Sky

SKILL LEVEL: EXPERIENCED

If you liked the Briargate pattern (page 144), you'll love this shawl. With similar construction and style, it's another great addition to your wardrobe.

## FINISHED MEASUREMENTS
- 80" wide × 21" deep (203.2 × 53.3cm)

## MATERIALS
- 440 yds (402.3m) fingering-weight yarn in Color A
- 440 yds (402.3m) fingering-weight yarn in Color B
- US Size 5 (3.75mm) circular needle, 32" (81.3cm) cable or longer, or size required for gauge
- Tapestry needle
- Blocking supplies

## YARN INFORMATION
- Sample uses Baby Boom from Fiesta Yarns (90% extra-fine superwash merino/10% nylon; 4oz/114g; 440 yds/402.3m), in color Great Horned Owl (Color A—1 skein) and Rain Maker (Color B—1 skein)

## GAUGE
- 20 sts and 36 rows = 4" (10.2cm) in St st, blocked
- *Gauge is not critical for this pattern; however, a different gauge will affect the finished size of the project as well as the amount of yarn needed.*

## PATTERN NOTES
- If using stitch markers to mark each stitch repeat, on some rows, the stitch markers will need to be rearranged. For this pattern, you'll need to rearrange these markers on Row 5 of the Chart. For more information on this technique, see page 14.

**The circular lace motif pairs nicely with the final edge detail.**

## INSTRUCTIONS

Work garter-tab CO as follows:

CO 3 sts. Knit 6 rows. Turn work 90-degrees clockwise, and pick up and knit 3 sts along the left edge. Turn work 90-degrees clockwise, and pick up and knit 3 sts from CO edge—9 sts total.

**Row 1 (RS):** Continue with Color A, k2, (yo, k1) to last 2 sts, yo, k2—15 sts.

**Row 2 (WS):** K3, yo, purl to last 3 sts, yo, k3—2 sts inc; 17 sts.

**Row 3:** K2, yo, knit to last 2 sts, yo, k2—2 sts inc; 19 sts.

Rep Rows 2 and 3 another 62 times—267 sts.

**Next Row (WS):** K3, yo, knit to last 3 sts, yo, k3—269 sts.

Knit 2 rows.

Cut Color A.

## LACE EDGING

With Color B and using the chart or written instructions, work Chart 3 times—365 sts.

Cut Color B, Color A will be used for remainder of shawl.

With Color A, work final edging as follows:

Knit 2 rows.

**Row 1 (RS):** K2, yo, knit to last 2 sts, yo, k2—367 sts.

**Row 2 (WS):** K3, yo, k2tog, knit to last 3 sts, yo, k3—368 sts.

**Row 3:** K1, *yo twice, sk2p; rep from * to last st, yo twice, k1.

**Row 4:** K1, *(k1, p1) twice into double yo, k1; rep from * to last 3 sts, (k1, p1) twice into double yo, k1.

| STITCH COUNTS FOR CHART A REPEATS | |
|---|---|
| First rep of Chart | 301 sts |
| Second rep of Chart | 333 sts |
| Third rep of Chart | 365 sts |

## Written Instructions for Chart

*Depending on what you prefer, follow either the chart or the written instructions below.*

**Row 1 (RS):** K2, yo, *k2, yo, ssk, k1, k2tog, yo, k1; rep from * to last 3 sts, k1, yo, k2.

**Row 2 and all even-numbered rows (WS):** K3, yo, purl to last 3 sts, yo, k3.

**Row 3:** K2, yo, k2, *k1, ssk, yo, k3, yo, k2tog; rep from * to last 5 sts, k3, yo, k2.

**Row 5:** K2, yo, k1, yo, k2, yo, *sk2p, yo, k2tog, yo, k1, yo, ssk, yo; rep from * to last 8 sts, sk2p, yo, k2, yo, k1, yo, k2.

**Row 7:** (K2, yo) twice, k3, yo, ssk, *k1, k2tog, yo, k3, yo, ssk; rep from * to last 10 sts, k1, k2tog, yo, k3, (yo, k2) twice.

**Row 9:** K2, (yo, k1) twice, *k2, yo, k2tog, k1, ssk, yo, k1; rep from * to last 5 sts, k2, yo, k1, yo, k2.

**Row 11:** K2, yo, k3, yo, k2tog, yo, *k1, yo, ssk, yo, sk2p, yo, k2tog, yo; rep from * to last 8 sts, k1, yo, ssk, yo, k3, yo, k2.

**Row 12:** K3, yo, purl to last 3 sts, yo, k3.

# FINISHING

BO loosely kwise on RS. Block shawl to finished
measurements given at beg of patt. With tapestry needle,
weave in ends.

## EARTH AND SKY CHART

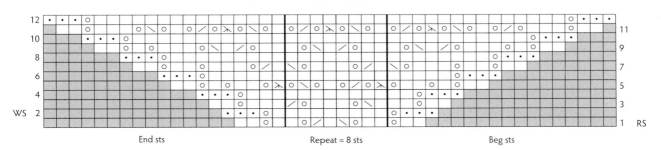

End sts   Repeat = 8 sts   Beg sts

## LEGEND

| | | | |
|---|---|---|---|
| ☐ | K on RS, P on WS | ╱ | K2tog |
| • | P on RS, K on WS | ⋏ | Sk2p |
| ╲ | Ssk | ▨ | No stitch |
| ○ | YO | | |

# Kelsey

An asymmetrical garter stitch shawl offers the ideal shape and texture to show off this cable-and-garter stitch pattern. Small bobbles accent the edge for extra texture.

## FINISHED MEASUREMENTS
- 70" wide × 22" deep (177.8 × 55.9cm)

## MATERIALS
- 570 yds (521.2m) sport-weight yarn
- US Size 5 (3.75mm) circular needle, 32" (81.3cm) cable or longer, or size required for gauge
- 1 stitch marker
- Cable needle
- Tapestry needle
- Blocking supplies

## YARN INFORMATION
- Sample uses 2 skeins of Yellowstone from Stitch Sprouts (80% wool/20% silk; 3.5oz/100g; 285 yds/260.6m) in color Reese Creek

## GAUGE
- 20 sts and 32 rows = 4" (10.2cm) in garter st, blocked
- *Gauge is not critical for this pattern; however, a different gauge will affect the finished size of the project as well as the amount of yarn needed.*

## SPECIAL ABBREVIATIONS
- **2/2 RC:** Sl 2 sts to cn, hold in back. K2, k2 from cn.
- **2/2 LC:** Sl 2 sts to cn, hold in front, K2, k2 from cn.
- **2/1 RPC:** Sl 1 st to cn, hold in back, K2, p1 from cn.
- **2/1 LPC:** Sl 2 sts to cn, hold in front, P1, k2 from cn.
- **MB:** Make bobble, work as follows: (K1, p1) 3 times into st, sl first 5 sts on RH needle over sixth st.

**Bobbles along the edge of the cable panel create texture at the edge of the shawl.**

## INSTRUCTIONS

CO 25 sts.

**Next Row (WS):** Knit all sts.

## BODY OF SHAWL

**Row 1 (RS):** K1, kfb, k1, k2tog, k1, pm, k19.

**Row 2 (WS):** K19, sm, knit to 2 sts before end, kfb, k1—26 sts.

**Row 3:** K1, kfb, knit to 3 sts before marker, k2tog, k1, sm, work Row 1 of Chart A to end.

**Row 4:** Work Row 2 of Chart A to marker, sm, knit to last 2 sts, kfb, k1—1 st inc in garter st section.

**Row 5:** K1, kfb, knit to 3 sts before marker, k2tog, k1, sm, work next row of Chart A to end.

**Row 6:** Work next row of Chart A to marker, sm, knit to last 2 sts, kfb, k1—1 st inc in garter st section.

Rep last two rows (working next row of Chart A, starting with Row 5) another 118 times (Chart A will be worked a total of 15 times)—146 sts; 127 in garter st section, 19 sts for Chart A.

Continue in established pattern for another 7 rows—149 sts; 130 sts in garter st section, 19 sts for Chart A.

**Next Row (WS):** Knit to marker, remove marker, knit to last 2 sts, kfb, k1—150 sts.

## Written Instructions for Chart A

*Depending on what you prefer, follow either the chart or the written instructions below.*

**Row 1 (RS):** K1, k2tog, yo, k2, p2, 2/2 RC, 2/2 LC, p2, k2.

**Row 2 (WS):** MB, k3, p8, k2, k2tog, yo, k3.

**Row 3:** K1, k2tog, yo, k2, p1, 2/1 RPC, p4, 2/1 LPC, p1, k2.

**Row 4:** K3, p10, k1, k2tog, yo, k3.

**Row 5:** K1, k2tog, yo, k2, p1, k2, p6, k2, o1, k2.

**Row 6:** MB, k2, p10, k1, k2tog, yo, k3.

**Row 7:** K1, k2tog, yo, k2, p1, 2/1 LPC, p4, 2/1 RPC, p1, k2.

**Row 8:** K4, p8, k2, k2tog, yo, k3.

**Row 9:** Rep Row 1.

# Make It Your Own!

Want a bigger shawl? You can have one! Repeat Rows 5 and 6 of the Body of Shawl section until you've worked Chart A an odd number of times (15, 17, 19, and so on) total. Then work the last 7 rows of the Body and Lace-Edging sections as written. Remember: If you make your shawl bigger, you'll need more yarn!

**Row 10:** Rep Row 2.

**Row 11:** K1, k2tog, yo, k2, p2, k8, p2, k2.

**Rows 12–15:** Rep Rows 8–11.

**Row 16:** Rep Row 8.

## LACE EDGING

Using the knitted cast on, CO 7 sts.

Using the chart or written instructions, work Chart B 74 times.

Work Rows 1–3 of Chart B once more.

### Written Instructions for Chart B

*Depending on what you prefer, follow either the chart or the written instructions below.*

**Row 1 (RS):** MB, k1, k2tog, yo, k2, ssk last border st with next body st on left needle, turn work.

**Row 2 (WS):** Sl1 wyib, k2tog, yo, k4, turn work.

**Row 3:** K2, k2tog, yo, k2, ssk the last border st with next body st on left needle, turn work.

**Row 4:** Rep Row 2, turn work.

## FINISHING

BO remaining sts on WS. Block shawl to finished measurements given at beg of patt. With tapestry needle, weave in ends.

## KELSEY CHART A

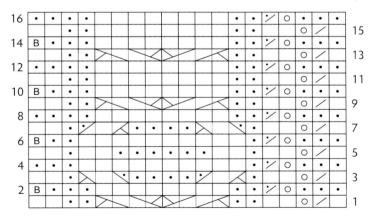

## KELSEY CHART B

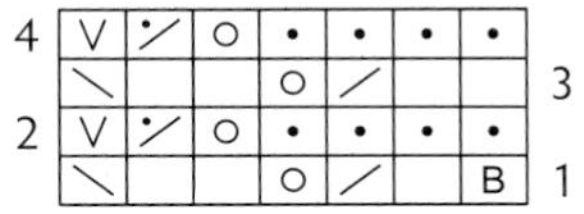

## LEGEND

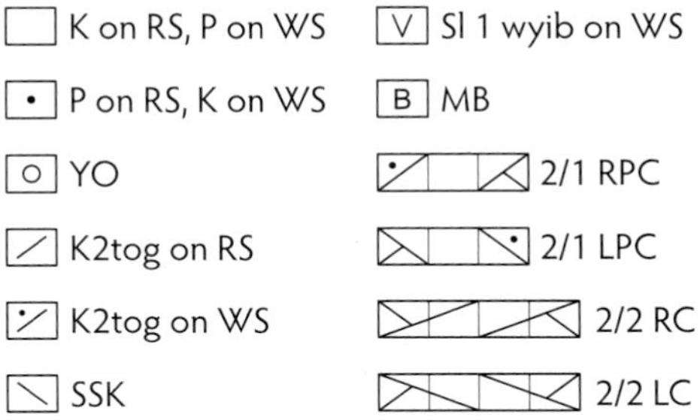

| | | | |
|---|---|---|---|
| ☐ K on RS, P on WS | | �_V Sl 1 wyib on WS | |
| • P on RS, K on WS | | B MB | |
| ○ YO | | 2/1 RPC | |
| ⁄ K2tog on RS | | 2/1 LPC | |
| ⁄ K2tog on WS | | 2/2 RC | |
| ＼ SSK | | 2/2 LC | |

# Wedgewood

Since we're making shawls knit with sock yarn, why not knit one that uses a common sock-knitting technique? The Wedgewood shawl is knit starting at the lace edge and features short rows to curve the shawl into a crescent shape.

## FINISHED MEASUREMENTS

- 78" wide × 10" deep (198.1 × 25.4cm)

## MATERIALS

- 430 yds (393.2m) worsted-weight yarn
- US Size 6 (4.0mm) circular needle, 32" (81.3cm) cable or longer, or size required for gauge
- Tapestry needle
- Blocking supplies

## YARN INFORMATION

- Sample uses 1 skein of Shepherd Sock from Lorna's Laces (80% superwash merino/20% nylon; 3.5oz/100g; 430 yds/393.2m) in color 310 Catalpa

## GAUGE

- 14 sts and 36 rows = 4" (10.2cm) in St st, blocked
- *Gauge is not critical for this pattern; however, a different gauge will affect the finished size of the project as well as the amount of yarn needed.*

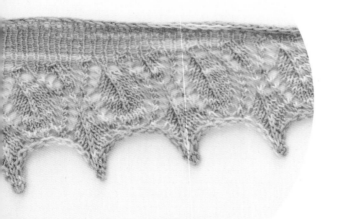

**A dramatic scalloped edge is the feature of this long, narrow shawl.**

## INSTRUCTIONS

CO 383 sts.

Knit 1 row on WS.

Using the chart or written instructions, work Chart—275 sts.

### Written Instructions for Chart

*Depending on what you prefer, follow either the chart or the written instructions below.*

**Row 1 (RS):** K2, k2tog, *k3, yo, ssk, yo, k1, yo, k2tog, yo, k3, CDD; rep from * to 15 sts from end, k3, yo, ssk, yo, k1, yo, k2tog, yo, k3, ssk, k2.

**Row 2 and all even-numbered rows (WS):** K2, purl to last 2 sts, k2.

**Row 3:** Rep Row 1.

**Row 5:** Rep Row 1.

**Row 7:** K2, k2tog, *k2, yo, k2tog, yo, k3, yo, ssk, yo, k2, CDD; rep from * to 15 sts from end, k2, yo, k2tog, yo, k3, yo, ssk, yo, k2, ssk, k2.

**Row 9:** K2, k2tog, *k1, yo, k2tog, yo, k5, yo, ssk, yo, k1, CDD; rep from * to 15 sts from end, k1, yo, k2tog, yo, k5, yo, ssk, yo, k1, ssk, k2.

**Row 11:** K2, k2tog, *yo, k2tog, yo, k7, yo, ssk, yo, CDD; rep from * to 15 sts from end, yo, k2tog, yo, k7, (yo, ssk) twice, k2.

**Rows 13:** K3, *yo, k2tog, yo, k3, CDD, k3, yo, ssk, yo, k1; rep from * to 16 sts from end, yo, k2tog, yo, k3, CDD, k3, yo, ssk, yo, k3.

**Row 15:** Rep Row 13.

**Row 17:** Rep Row 13.

**Row 19:** K3, *k1, yo, ssk, yo, k2, CDD, k2, yo, k2tog, yo, k2; rep from * to 16 sts from end, k1, yo, ssk, yo, k2, CDD, k2, yo, k2tog, yo, k4.

**Row 21:** K2, k2tog, *k1, yo, ssk, yo, k1, CDD, k1, yo, k2tog, yo, k1, CDD; rep from * to 15 sts from end, k1, yo, ssk, yo, k1, CDD, k1, yo, k2tog, yo, k1, ssk, k2.

**Row 23:** K2, k2tog, *k1, yo, ssk, yo, CDD, yo, k2tog, yo, k1, CDD; rep from * to 13 sts from end, k1, yo, ssk, yo, CDD, yo, k2tog, yo, k1, ssk, k2.

**Row 24:** K2, purl to last 2 sts, k2.

## SHORT-ROW BODY

**Row 1 (RS):** K144, turn work.

**Row 2 (WS):** P13, turn work.

**Row 3:** K12, ssk, k3, turn work—274 sts.

**Row 4:** P15, p2tog, p3, turn work—273 sts.

**Row 5:** Knit to 1 st before gap (1 st before previous turning point), ssk, k3, turn work.

**Row 6:** Purl to 1 st before gap, p2tog, p3, turn work.

Rep Rows 5 and 6 another 30 times—211 sts; 3 sts remain unworked at each edge.

**Next Row (RS):** Knit to last 4 sts, ssk, k2—210 sts.

# FINISHING

BO loosely kwise on WS. Block shawl to finished measurements given at beg of patt. With tapestry needle, weave in ends.

## WEDGEWOOD CHART

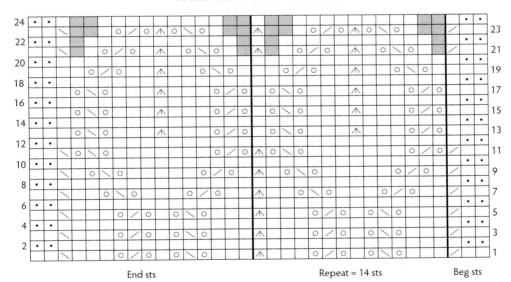

End sts      Repeat = 14 sts      Beg sts

## LEGEND

| | | | |
|---|---|---|---|
| ☐ | K on RS, P on WS | ⋏ | CDD |
| ⟋ | K2tog | • | P on RS, K on WS |
| ⊙ | YO | ▨ | No stitch |
| ⟍ | Ssk | | |

# Floe

Here's another short-row shawl with a twist. The border is worked sideways, with stitches for the body of the shawl being added along the side of the border as you go with wraps and turns—a fun new way to work a lace border!

## FINISHED MEASUREMENTS

- 68" wide × 15" deep (172.7 × 38.1cm)

## MATERIALS

- 400 yds (365.8m) fingering-weight yarn in Color A
- 400 yds (365.8m) fingering-weight yarn in Color B
- US Size 4 (3.5mm) circular needle, 32" (81.3cm) cable or longer, or size required for gauge
- 1 stitch marker
- Tapestry needle
- Blocking supplies

## YARN INFORMATION

- Sample uses Caper Sock from String Theory Hand Dyed Yarn (80% superwash merino/10% cashmere/10% nylon; 4oz/113g; 400 yds/365.8m) in color Brina (Color A—1 skein) and Agave (Color B—1 skein).

## GAUGE

- 16 sts and 36 rows = 4" (10.2cm) in St st, blocked
- *Gauge is not critical for this pattern; however, a different gauge will affect the finished size of the project as well as the amount of yarn needed.*

## SPECIAL ABBREVIATIONS

- **w&t:** Move yarn to front, slip next st purlwise to RH needle, move yarn to back, move st back to LH needle, turn.

## PATTERN NOTES

- When working Rows 5 and 6 of the Lace-Edging section, you are working the next row of the Chart with each repeat. This means you are repeating the Chart while, **at the same time**, working the instructions given in Rows 5 and 6.

**Colorwork and short rows create drama.**

## INSTRUCTIONS

Begin shawl by working lace border as follows.

## LACE EDGING

With Color A, CO 23 sts.

**Row 1 (RS):** Kfb, pm, knit to end—24 sts.

**Row 2 (WS):** Knit to marker, sm, k1, w&t, turn work.

**Row 3:** Kfb, sm, work Row 1 of Chart to end.

**Row 4:** Work Row 2 of Chart to marker, sm, k1, w&t, turn work, leaving remaining sts unworked.

**Row 5:** K1f&b, SM, work next row of chart to end.

**Row 6:** Work next row of chart to marker, sm, k1, w&t, turn work, leaving remaining sts unworked.

Rep last two rows, working subsequent row of Chart each row, until Chart is repeated 17 times total, ending with Row 36 of Chart—330 sts, 22 sts on one side of stitch marker, 308 sts on the other.

**Next row (RS):** K1, SM, knit to end.

BO 23 sts on WS, removing marker—307 sts.

## Written Instructions for Chart

*Depending on what you prefer, follow either the chart or the written instructions below.*

**Row 1 (RS):** K2, yo, k2, ssk, k4, k2tog, k2, yo, k1, (yo, ssk) twice, yo, k3.

**Row 2 (WS):** K2, p21.

**Row 3:** K3, yo, k2, ssk, k2, k2tog, k2, yo, k3, (yo, ssk) twice, yo, k3.

**Row 4:** K2, p22.

**Row 5:** K2, yo, ssk, yo, k2, ssk, k2tog, k2, yo, k5, (yo, ssk) twice, yo, k3.

**Row 6:** K2, p23.

**Row 7:** K3, yo, ssk, yo, k2, ssk, k4, k2tog, k2, yo, k1, (yo, ssk) twice, yo, k3.

**Row 8:** K2, p24.

**Row 9:** K2, (yo, ssk) twice, yo, k2, ssk, k2, k2tog, k2, yo, k3, (yo, ssk) twice, yo, k3.

**Row 10:** K2, p25.

**Row 11:** K3, (yo, ssk) twice, yo, k2, ssk, k2tog, k2, yo, k5, (yo, ssk) twice, yo, k3.

**Row 12:** K2, p26.

**Row 13:** K4, (yo, ssk) twice, yo, k2, ssk, k4, k2tog, k2, yo, k1, (yo, ssk) twice, yo, k3.

**Row 14:** K2, p27.

**Row 15:** K3, (yo, ssk) 3 times, yo, k2, ssk, k2, k2tog, k2, yo, k3, (yo, ssk) twice, yo, k3.

**Row 16:** K2, p28.

**Row 17:** K4, (yo, ssk) 3 times, yo, k2, ssk, k2tog, k2, yo, k5, (yo, ssk) twice, yo, k3.

**Row 18:** K2, p29.

**Row 19:** K2tog, k2, yo, (k2tog, yo) 3 times, k1, yo, k2, ssk, k4, k2tog, k2, (yo, k2tog) 3 times, k2.

**Row 20:** K2, p28.

**Row 21:** K3, (k2tog, yo) 3 times, k3, yo, k2, ssk, k2, k2tog, k2, (yo, k2tog) 3 times, k2.

**Row 22:** K2, p27.

**Row 23:** K2, (k2tog, yo) 3 times, k5, yo, k2, ssk, k2tog, k2, (yo, k2tog) 3 times, k2.

**Row 24:** K2, p26.

**Row 25:** K1, (k2tog, yo) 3 times, k1, yo, k2, ssk, k4, k2tog, k2, (yo, k2tog) 3 times, k2.

**Row 26:** K2, p25.

**Row 27:** K2, (k2tog, yo) twice, k3, yo, k2, ssk, k2, k2tog, k2, (yo, k2tog) 3 times, k2.

**Row 28:** K2, p24.

**Row 29:** K1, (k2tog, yo) twice, k5, yo, k2, ssk, k2tog, k2, (yo, k2tog) 3 times, k2.

**Row 30:** K2, p23.

**Row 31:** K2, k2tog, yo, k1, yo, k2, ssk, k4, k2tog, k2, (yo, k2tog) 3 times, k2.

**Row 32:** K2, p22.

**Row 33:** K1, k2tog, yo, k3, yo, k2, ssk, k2, k2tog, k2, (yo, k2tog) 3 times, k2.

**Row 34:** K2, p21.

**Row 35:** K7, yo, k2, ssk, k2tog, k2, (yo, k2tog) 3 times, k2.

**Row 36:** K2, p20.

## SHORT-ROW BODY

**Set-Up Row (WS):** With A, K2, K2tog, knit to last 4 sts, K2tog, K2—305 sts.

Cut Color A. Use Color B for remainder of shawl.

**Row 1 (RS):** With Color B, k157, turn work.

**Row 2 (WS):** P9, turn work.

**Row 3:** K8, ssk, k3, turn work—304 sts.

**Row 4:** P11, p2tog, p3, turn work—303 sts.

**Row 5:** Knit to 1 st before gap (1 st before previous turning point), ssk, k3, turn work.

**Row 6:** Purl to 1 st before gap (1 st before previous turning point), p2tog, p3, turn work.

Work last two rows another 35 times—231 sts; all sts have been worked.

Knit 6 rows.

## FINISHING

BO loosely kwise on RS. Block shawl to finished measurements given at beg of patt. With tapestry needle, weave in ends.

## FLOE CHART

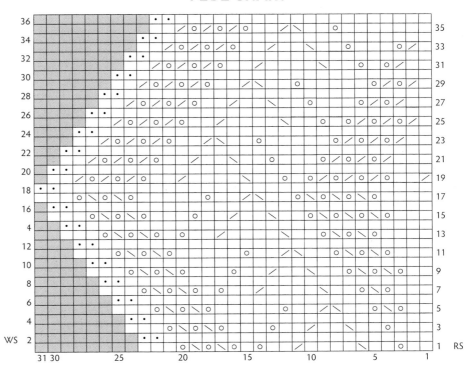

### LEGEND

- ☐ K on RS, P on WS
- • P on RS, K on WS
- ⟍ Ssk
- ⊙ YO
- ⟋ K2tog
- ▨ No stitch

# Lake Delton

I named this design after the place my family has been vacationing in Wisconsin for the last two decades. We love spending long weekends at the lake, enjoying family time at the beach. This shawl is perfect for those cool nights sitting lakeside, recounting stories of our childhood.

## FINISHED MEASUREMENTS

- 84" wide × 28" deep (213.4 × 71.1cm)

## MATERIALS

- 800 yds (731.5m) fingering-weight yarn
- US Size 5 (3.75mm) circular needle, 24" (61cm) cable or longer, or size needed to obtain gauge
- Tapestry needle
- Blocking supplies

## YARN INFORMATION

- Sample uses 2 skeins of Caper Sock from String Theory Hand Dyed Yarn (80% superwash merino/10% cashmere/10% nylon; 4oz/113g; 400 yds/365.8m) in the color Jade

## GAUGE

- 20 sts and 28 rows = 4" (10.2cm) in St st, blocked
- *Gauge is not critical for this pattern; however, a different gauge will affect the finished size of the project as well as the amount of yarn needed.*

**An interesting eight-row lace panel is knitted onto the body of the shawl, adding a lovely, delicate detail to the edge.**

## INSTRUCTIONS

Work garter-tab CO as follows:

CO 2 sts. Knit 24 rows. Turn work 90-degrees clockwise, and pick up and knit 12 sts along the left edge. Turn work 90-degrees clockwise, and pick up and knit 2 sts from CO edge—16 sts total.

**Set-Up Row (WS):** Knit all sts.

**Row 1 (RS):** K2, (yo, k1) 6 times, (k1, yo) 6 times, k2—28 sts.

**Row 2:** K2, purl to last 2 sts, k2.

**Row 3:** Knit all sts.

**Row 4:** Rep Row 2.

**Row 5:** K3, (yo, k1) 11 times, (k1, yo) 11 times, k3—50 sts.

**Row 6:** Knit all sts.

## BODY OF SHAWL

Using the chart or written instructions, work Chart A 13 times—258 sts.

Work Rows 1–7 of Chart A once more—272 sts

**Next Row (WS):** Knit all sts.

### Written Instructions for Chart A

*Depending on what you prefer, follow either the chart or the written instructions below.*

**Row 1 (RS):** K2, yo, k1, k2tog, *yo twice, ssk, k2tog; rep from * to last 5 sts, yo twice, ssk, k1, yo, k2.

**Row 2 (WS):** K3, yo, *p2, (k1, p1) into double yo; rep from * to last 5 sts, p2, yo, k3.

| STITCH COUNTS FOR BODY OF SHAWL | |
|---|---|
| First rep of Chart A | 66 sts |
| Second rep of Chart A | 82 sts |
| Third rep of Chart A | 98 sts |
| Fourth rep of Chart A | 114 sts |
| Fifth rep of Chart A | 130 sts |
| Sixth rep of Chart A | 146 sts |
| Seventh rep of Chart A | 162 sts |
| Eighth rep of Chart A | 178 sts |
| Ninth rep of Chart A | 194 sts |
| Tenth rep of Chart A | 210 sts |
| Eleventh rep of Chart A | 226 sts |
| Twelfth rep of Chart A | 242 sts |
| Thirteenth rep of Chart A | 258 sts |
| Final Rows 1–7 of Chart A | 272 sts |

**Row 3:** K2, yo, knit to last 2 sts, yo, k2.

**Row 4:** K3, yo, purl to last 3 sts, yo, k3.

**Row 5:** K2, yo, k1, yo, *ssk, k2tog, yo twice; rep from * to last 7 sts, ssk, k2tog, yo, k1, yo, k2.

**Row 6:** K3, yo, p4, (k1, p1) into double yo, p2; rep from * to last 5 sts, p2, yo, k3.

**Row 7:** Rep Row 3.

**Row 8:** Rep Row 4.

Rep Rows 1–8 for patt.

# Make It Your Own!

Have two favorite skeins of yarn? Use one skein for the body of the shawl and one for the lace edge to create a beautiful two-color shawl. Make sure each skein contains at least 400 yds (365.8m) of yarn.

## LACE EDGING

With RS facing and using the knitted cast on, CO 22 sts.

**Row 1 (RS):** K21, ssk last border st with first body st on left needle, turn.

**Row 2 (WS):** Sl1 wyib, k21, turn.

Rep Rows 1 and 2 once more.

Using the chart or written instructions, work Chart B 67 times.

Rep Rows 1 and 2.

Rep Row 1 once more.

## Written Instructions for Chart B

*Depending on what you prefer, follow either the chart or the written instructions below.*

**Row 1 (RS):** K4, k2tog twice, (YO, k1) 3 times, YO, ssk twice, k6, ssk last border st with next body st on left needle, turn.

**Row 2 and all even-numbered rows (WS):** Sl1 wyib, K2, p17, k2, turn.

**Row 3:** K3, k2tog twice, yo, k1, yo, k3, yo, k1, yo, ssk twice, k5, ssk last border st with next body st on left needle, turn.

**Row 5:** K6, k2tog twice, (yo, k1) 3 times, yo, ssk twice, k4, ssk last border st with next body st on left needle, turn.

**Row 7:** K5, k2tog twice, yo, K1, yo, K3, yo, K1, yo, ssk twice, k3, ssk last border st with next body st on left needle, turn.

**Row 8:** Sl1 wyib, k2, p17, k2, turn.

Rep Rows 1–8 for patt.

## FINISHING

BO loosely kwise on WS. Block shawl to finished measurements given at beg of patt. With tapestry needle, weave in ends.

### LAKE DELTON CHART A

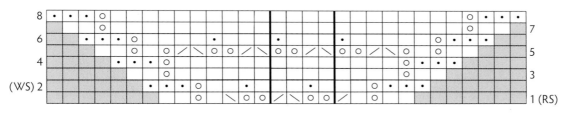

Repeat = 4 sts

### LEGEND

| | | | |
|---|---|---|---|
| ☐ K on RS, P on WS | | ○ YO | |
| • P on RS, K on WS | | ╱ K2tog | |
| ▨ No stitch | | ╲ Ssk | |

### LAKE DELTON CHART B

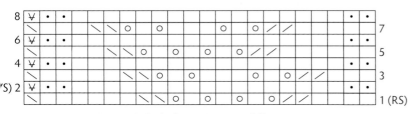

Work final ssk on RS rows as follows:
ssk last border st with next body st on left needle.

### LEGEND

| | |
|---|---|
| ☐ K on RS, P on WS | ╲ Ssk |
| • P on RS, K on WS | ○ YO |
| ╱ K2tog | ⱶ Sl 1 wyib on WS |

# Daylily

Leaf motifs and feather and fan come together to make this stunning circular pi shawl. This project is great as either a shawl or a baby blanket!

## FINISHED MEASUREMENTS

- 54" (137.2cm) in diameter

## MATERIALS

- 1,150 yds (1,052m) fingering-weight yarn
- US Size 5 (3.75 mm) double-pointed needles, or size needed to obtain gauge
- US Size 5 (3.75 mm) circular needle, 24" (61cm) cable, or size needed to obtain gauge
- US Size 5 (3.75 mm) circular needle, 32" (81.3cm) cable or longer, or size needed to obtain gauge
- 1 stitch marker
- Tapestry needle
- Blocking supplies

## YARN INFORMATION

- Sample uses 5 balls of Capretta Superwash from Knit Picks (80% merino superwash/10% cashmere/10% nylon; 1.8oz/50g; 230 yds/210.3m) in the color Hunter

## GAUGE

- 20 sts and 24 rows = 4" (10.2cm) in St st, blocked
- *Gauge is not critical for this pattern; however, a different gauge will affect the finished size of the project as well as the amount of yarn needed.*

## PATTERN NOTES

- If using stitch markers to mark each stitch repeat, on some rows, the stitch markers will need to be rearranged. For this pattern, you'll need to rearrange these stitch markers on Rows 1, 3, and 5 for Chart A, and Row 9 for Chart C. For more information on this technique, see page 14.
- Instructions include "at the same time" directions for moving the beginning of round stitch marker at the end of some rounds for some of the charts. Take care not to miss those!

**The feather and fan pattern gives the shawl a beautiful, pointed edge.**

## INSTRUCTIONS

With double-pointed needles and using circular cast on (page 13), CO 9 sts.

Pm and join sts in the round.

Knit 1 rnd.

**Inc Rnd:** (Yo, k1) around—18 sts.

Knit 2 rnds.

**Next Rnd:** K1, m1, k10, m1, knit to end of rnd—20 sts.

## SECTION 1 (8 ROUNDS)

**Inc Rnd:** (Yo, k1) around—40 sts.

**Next Rnd:** Knit all sts.

Using the chart or the written instructions for the chart, work Chart A, while **at the same time**, on even rnds, remove marker at end of rnd, k1, pm, this marks new start of rnd.

### Written Instructions for Chart A

*Depending on what you prefer, follow either the chart or the written instructions below.*

**Rnd 1:** *K3, yo, k1, yo, k3, sk2p; rep from * around.

**Rnd 2:** Knit all sts. At end of rnd, remove marker, k1, pm to mark new start of rnd.

**Rnd 3:** *K2, yo, k3, yo, k2, sk2p; rep from * around.

**Rnd 4:** Knit all sts. At end of rnd, remove marker, k1, pm to mark new start of rnd.

**Rnd 5:** *(K1, yo) twice, sk2p, (yo, k1) twice, sk2p; rep from * around.

**Rnd 6:** Knit all sts. At end of rnd, remove marker, k1, pm to mark new start of rnd.

## SECTION 2 (16 ROUNDS)

**Inc Rnd:** (Yo, k1) around—80 sts.

**Next Rnd:** Knit all sts.

Using the chart or the written instructions for the chart, work Chart B.

# Make It Bigger!

With extra yarn, Chart E can be repeated to desired length.

## Written Instructions for Chart B

*Depending on what you prefer, follow either the chart or the written instructions below.*

**Rnd 1:** *Yo, ssk, k2tog, yo, k1; rep from * around.
**Rnd 2 and all even-numbered rnds:** Knit all sts.
**Rnd 3:** *K1, yo, ssk, k3, k2tog, yo, k2; rep from * around.
**Rnd 5:** *K2, yo, ssk, k1, k2tog, yo, k3; rep from * around.
**Rnd 7:** *K3, yo, sk2p, yo, k4; rep from * around.
**Rnds 9, 11, and 13:** *Ssk, k2, yo, k1, yo, k2, k2tog, k1; rep from * around.
**Rnd 14:** Knit all sts.

## SECTION 3 (32 ROUNDS)

*Note: Transfer to 24" (61cm) circular needle when stitches no longer comfortably fit on the double-pointed needles.*

**Inc Rnd:** (Yo, k1) around—160 sts.
**Next Rnd:** Knit all sts.
Using the chart or the written instructions for the chart, work Chart C 3 times, while **at the same time**, on Rnd 8 of Chart C, remove marker at end of rnd, k1, pm, this marks new start of rnd.

## Written Instructions for Chart C

*Depending on what you prefer, follow either the chart or the written instructions below.*

**Rnd 1:** *K4, yo, ssk, k4; rep from * around.
**Rnds 2, 4, and 6:** Knit all sts.
**Rnd 3:** *K2, k2tog, yo, k1, yo, ssk, k3; rep from * around.
**Rnd 5:** *K1, k2tog, yo, k3, yo, ssk, k2; rep from * around.
**Rnd 7:** *K2tog, yo, k5, yo, ssk, k1; rep from * around.
**Rnd 8:** Knit all sts. At end of rnd, remove marker, k1, pm to mark new start of rnd.
**Rnd 9:** *Yo, k7, yo, sk2p; rep from * around.
**Rnd 10:** Knit all sts.

## SECTION 4 (50 ROUNDS)

*Note: Transfer to 32" (81.3cm) or longer circular needle when sts no longer comfortably fit on current needles.*

**Inc Rnd:** (Yo, k1) around—320 sts.
**Next Rnd:** Knit all sts.
Using the chart or the written instructions for the chart, work Chart D 4 times.

## Written Instructions for Chart D

*Depending on what you prefer, follow either the chart or the written instructions below.*

**Rnd 1:** *Yo, ssk, k5, k2tog, yo, k1; rep from * around.
**Rnd 2 and all even-numbered rnds:** Knit all sts.
**Rnd 3:** *K1, yo, ssk, k3, k2tog, yo, k2; rep from * around.
**Rnd 5:** *K2, yo, ssk, k1, k2tog, yo, k3; rep from * around.
**Rnd 7:** *K1, yo, ssk, yo, sk2p, yo, k2tog, yo, k2; rep from * around.
**Rnd 9:** *K2, yo, ssk, k1, k2tog, yo, k3; rep from * around.
**Rnd 11:** *K3, yo, sk2p, yo, k4; rep from * around.
**Rnd 12:** Knit all sts.

## SECTION 5 (41 ROUNDS)

**Inc Rnd:** (Yo, k1) around—640 sts.
**Next Rnd:** Knit all sts.
Using the chart or the written instructions for the chart, work Chart E 9 times.
Work Rnds 1–3 of Chart E once more.

## Written Instructions for Chart E

*Depending on what you prefer, follow either the chart or the written instructions below.*

**Rnds 1 and 2:** Knit all sts.
**Rnd 3:** *K2tog 3 times, (k1, yo) 6 times, k1, ssk 3 times, k1; rep from * around.
**Rnd 4:** Knit all sts.

## FINISHING

BO loosely kwise. Block shawl to finished measurements given at beg of patt. With tapestry needle, weave in ends.

## DAYLILY CHART A

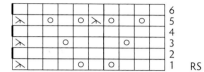

## DAYLILY CHART B

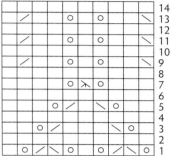

## DAYLILY CHART C

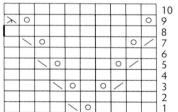

## DAYLILY CHART D

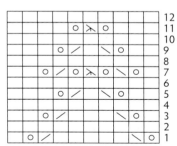

## DAYLILY CHART E

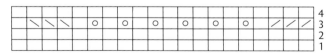

## LEGEND

| | | | |
|---|---|---|---|
| ☐ | K on RS, P on WS | ◲ | Ssk |
| ⊡ | YO | ◿ | K2tog |
| ⋌ | Sk2p | ❘ | Remove marker, K1, PM |

# Knitting Abbreviations

**\*** repeat instructions following the single asterisk as directed.

**\*\*** repeat instructions following the asterisks as directed.

**"** inch(es)

**1/1 RC** slip 1 to cable needle, hold in back, knit 1, knit 1 from cable needle

**2/2 RC** slip 2 stitches to cable needle, hold in back, knit 2, knit 2 from cable needle

**2/2 LC** slip 2 stitches to cable needle, hold in front, knit 2, knit 2 from cable needle

**2/1 RPC** slip 1 stitch to cable needle, hold in back, knit 2, purl 1 from cable needle

**2/1 LPC** slip 2 stitches to cable needle, hold in front, purl 1, knit 2 from cable needle

**beg** begin(ning)

**BO** bind off

**CDD** slip 2 stitches together as if to knit 2 together, knit 1 stitch, pass the 2 slipped stitches over the knit stitch—2 stitches decreased

**cn** cable needle(s)

**CO** cast on

**g** gram(s)

**inc(s)** increase(ing)(s)

**k** knit

**kfb** knit into front and back of same stitch—1 stitch increased

**k2tog** knit 2 stitches together—1 stitch decreased

**kwise** knitwise

**LH** left hand

**m** meter(s)

**m1** with left-hand needle, pick up bar between needles, bringing needle from front to back, and knit into back of stitch—1 stitch increased

**MB** make bobble—(knit 1, purl 1) three times into stitch, slip first 5 stitches on right-hand needle over sixth stitch

**mm** millimeter(s)

**oz** ounce(s)

**p** purl

**patt(s)** pattern(s)

**p2tog** purl 2 stitches together—1 stitch decreased

**pm** place marker

**pwise** purlwise

**rem** remain(ing)

**rep(s)** repeat(s)

**RH** right hand

**rnd(s)** round(s)

**RS** right side

**sk2p** slip 1 knitwise, knit 2 together, pass slipped stitch over the knit 2 together—2 stitches decreased

**sl** slip stitch(es)— slip stitches purlwise unless instructed otherwise

**sm** slip marker

**ssk** slip 2 stitches knitwise, 1 at a time, to right needle, then insert left needle from left to right into front loops and knit 2 stitches together—1 stitch decreased

**sssk** slip 3 stitches knitwise, 1 at a time, to right needle, then insert left needle from left to right into front loops and knit 3 stitches together—2 stitches decreased

**st(s)** stitch(es)

**St st** stockinette stitch

**tbl** through back loop(s)

**tog** together

**w&t** move yarn to front, slip next stitch purlwise to right-hand needle, move yarn to back, move st back to left-hand needle, turn

**WS** wrong side

**wyib** with yarn in back

**wyif** with yarn in front

**yd(s)** yard(s)

**yo(s)** yarn over(s)

# Index

# About the Author

**Jen Lucas** has been knitting for over 20 years. She has designed hundreds of knitting and crochet patterns for yarn companies, magazines, and books in addition to her dozens of self-published designs. Jen is the author of many knitting books, including the best seller *Sock-Yarn Shawls*. She lives in Northern Illinois with her husband, Alex, and a home full of crafts. Learn more about Jen at craftyjencrafts.com.

## ACKNOWLEDGMENTS

There are so many people to thank for this book. To all the shawl makers out there, thank you. It has seriously been an absolute joy watching you make my patterns, seeing you in the many classes I've taught over the years, and engaging with me in online. I look forward to seeing where we go together next.

Thank you to Fox Chapel Publishing for making this book a reality. I never dreamed I would get to do a book like this, and I appreciate the entire team's work on this endeavor and bringing these patterns back to life. And many thanks to the former Martingale & Company team. I'm proud of the books we created together, and I'm beyond thrilled that the books I created with you can continue on in a new way with Fox Chapel.

Thank you, as always, to my husband, Alex. Your encouragement and support and general awesomeness make all of this possible. I couldn't do this without you.